# A History of
# Women's Lives on
# the Isle of Wight

# A History of Women's Lives on the Isle of Wight

Daisy Plant

PEN & SWORD
HISTORY

AN IMPRINT OF PEN & SWORD BOOKS LTD.
YORKSHIRE - PHILADELPHIA

First published in Great Britain in 2019 by
Pen & Sword Military
An imprint of
Pen & Sword Books Ltd
Yorkshire – Philadelphia

Copyright © Daisy Plant, 2019

ISBN 978 1 52672 0 290

The right of Daisy Plant to be identified as Author of this
work has been asserted by her in accordance with the Copyright,
Designs and Patents Act 1988.

Printed and bound in England by TJ International, Padstow, Cornwall

Pen & Sword Books Limited incorporates the imprints of Atlas, Archaeology,
Aviation, Discovery, Family History, Fiction, History, Maritime, Military,
Military Classics, Politics, Select, Transport, True Crime, Air World,
Frontline Publishing, Leo Cooper, Remember When, Seaforth Publishing,
The Praetorian Press, Wharncliffe Local History, Wharncliffe Transport,
Wharncliffe True Crime and White Owl.

For a complete list of Pen & Sword titles please contact

PEN & SWORD BOOKS LIMITED
47 Church Street, Barnsley, South Yorkshire, S70 2AS, England
E-mail: enquiries@pen-and-sword.co.uk
Website: www.pen-and-sword.co.uk

Or

PEN AND SWORD BOOKS
1950 Lawrence Rd, Havertown, PA 19083, USA
E-mail: Uspen-and-sword@casematepublishers.com
Website: www.penandswordbooks.com

*For Nanny, without whom this book would be far shorter. I wish you could be here to see it.*

# Contents

# Introduction

A lot can happen in the span of a hundred years.

Imagine being born a woman in the year 1850, on a little island off the south coast of England, in an even smaller seaside town. You would probably be one of several children – the average number at this time was six. You would not go to school.

You would learn to sew and to cook, most likely from your mother. You would help to look after any brothers and sisters younger than you. When you were older, perhaps 15, you might find a job. Many girls went into domestic service – that is, working as maids or cooks in bigger, more affluent households than their own. But this would not be expected to be a permanent position, and by the time you were 25 you would be married.

You would have children. It would be your duty to raise them, to buy their food and clothes with your husband's money, to care for them and keep them entertained. You might make a little extra cash sewing dresses and hats to sell, but your first priority would be to your children and to your husband.

This was by no means a bad life. Many women enjoyed it and were happy. Many more choose to live such lives today. But that is the key difference between our time and theirs; today's women have the ability to choose.

Now, imagine you were born in 1950, in that same little town on that same little island. You would be legally required to attend school and, thanks to The Education Act that came into play in 1947, you would not be allowed to leave until you were 15. Beach holidays were at their height in the UK in the 1950s and 1960s, and the Isle of Wight would have been a popular tourist attraction.

There would be a greater range of jobs available to you as a woman when you left school than there would have been for a girl of the same age born in 1850. You would still be expected to eventually marry and give up your career to devote your time to your family, but there was less pressure to marry as young. The mysterious diseases that would have stolen your loved ones away a century before were now mostly treatable.

Contraception was legalised in the UK in 1961 for married women, and extended to all others in 1967. This year also marked the introduction of The Abortion Act, which made it legal to terminate a pregnancy up to twenty-eight weeks gestation. This meant that you would be able to have sex without having to worry about falling pregnant, or the potential stress of an illegal abortion – which were often incredibly dangerous. A study done in 2010 found that the average number of children in a family was now likely to be nearer two, with only one in ten of the women asked having four or more.

This book aims to take you on a journey, following the lives of women living on the Isle of Wight in 1850 all the way through the next hundred years. We'll see both world wars. We'll watch women fight to change legislation and win rights they'd previously been denied – to divorce, to keep their children, to work, and to vote. We'll watch them love and hate, be aggressive, be passive, promiscuous and prim, quiet and loud. Because every woman is different; every woman *was* different, and while we can never meet them all, hopefully this book will provide a window into their world.

# CHAPTER ONE

# Education

School was not compulsory for children in the UK until 1880, when a combination of factors (predominantly the fact that working conditions were terrible, and employers could get away with paying children a lot less than adults because they couldn't complain to anyone about it) led to the agreement that it was best for the general populace if children between the ages of 5 and 10 years old were required to complete some form of education

Prior to this, a school education was possible, but realistically only given to children from well-off families. Working-class children were expected to go to work from an early age (depending on the nature of the job, some were sent out to work as soon as they could walk), with their earnings contributing to the family's income and helping the household to stay afloat. On the Isle of Wight, many children would have found themselves working in the shipyard, selling wares on the street, climbing up chimneys, or helping out on farms (often as bird scarers, who were paid to act as human scarecrows and keep crops safe from pests).

Girls would be taught needlework and domestic skills by their mothers (or, in the absence of a mother, a mother-like figure. Many women died young of illness or of complications as a result of childbirth, and their husbands would often remarry). These skills would serve her for the rest of her life. Children were also known to take in and do laundry for money, and girls often took on apprenticeships with dressmakers and milliners.

Because of all this, many parents were incredibly upset when the 1870 Education Act made it a legal requirement for children to attend school, with the age of attendance set by an elected school board. If children were at school, then they were not out earning a wage. Furthermore, parents had to pay for their children to attend school, and were subject to fines or even imprisonment if they didn't show up. Despite the likely repercussions, however, truancy was still a real problem. Many employers were willing to turn a blind eye and continued to pay child workers, who were paid a lower wage than their older colleagues.

Recent government statistics (autumn 2016 – spring 2017) indicate that absences were higher among low-income families, with children entitled to and claiming free school meals attaining an overall absence rate of 7 per cent compared to 4 per cent of children not claiming free school meals.

Although the reasons may have differed slightly, one would expect to find similar trends dating back throughout our time period.

Older children were needed at home to care for younger siblings – remember, it wasn't unusual to have both a teenager and a toddler at once, there could be so many children in a family – if they weren't working. Parents of children affected by the 1870 Education Act probably would not have attended school themselves, and so would not have seen much of a point to it – they were still alive, they had jobs, they weren't starving, so what good was a school education going to be for their children? The most recent studies in the UK have shown that factors such as exam stress now have much more of an impact on absences in schools than they would have done in the 1870s, with many children and teenagers today finding that the pressure put on them to make good grades creates high levels of anxiety and depression. Back then, the mentality among many working-class families was that a child only needed to learn how to read, write, and do basic mathematics at school. Children would have seen their parents struggling to make ends meet, and many would have wanted to work so that they could help with that. The fact that they were legally barred from doing so was frustrating and upsetting to many. Furthermore, children adopt the opinions and beliefs of their parents, particularly when they are young. If their parents hadn't gone to school and didn't see the point in sending their children, then the children would believe that this was the right attitude to have. There was no point in going, because their parents had jobs and they hadn't gone.

As late as 1902, children were missing school so that they could help with siblings or earn extra money for the household. A man called John Lockhart was summoned to court on the Isle of Wight because his daughter Minnie 'had made 14 attendances out of a possible 27'. The attendance officer had seen her out and about with a baby in a pram. In the end, the chairman explained that it was illegal 'to keep the child at home to look after younger children'. They were given a month to fix the issue.

There are many cases like this in the petty sessions section of the newspaper, often with parents saying that they sent their children to school but that the children just didn't go. Corporal punishment wasn't abolished in English schools until long after 1950; one has to wonder how much of an impact this would have had in scaring children into playing truant.

In 1880, the leaving age was set nationally at 10 years old, and the fees were abolished in state schools. This Act also saw the introduction of attendance officers, who were sent to check on households where the children were truant, possibly arresting the parents if they deemed a child's absence unnecessary. Again, working-class families were most affected by this change in law, and attendance officers were known to frequent the more impoverished areas of the island in search of absentee children.

In 1893, the school-leaving age was raised to 11, and a mandatory education was extended to include deaf and blind children, with the requirement that provisions were in place to make learning accessible to them. Although these might have been somewhat primitive methods by today's standards, it was a huge step in allowing disabled and disadvantaged children the same chances as their able-bodied counterparts. We still have quite a way to go in this respect, with a study conducted as recently as 2018 finding that there were far too few specialist teaching staff available to teach a growing number of deaf pupils.

In 1918, the Fisher Education Act raised the leaving age to 14. It also capped class sizes at a maximum of thirty pupils, which would have greatly improved the quality of learning as it would mean a teacher could focus on the needs of each individual student; in larger classes this becomes difficult.

The government had plans to raise the leaving age to 15 in 1939, although these were delayed by the Second World War and did not come into effect until 1947.

Doing well at school brought with it the opportunity for new, better paid careers in the future. Teaching was an occupation pursued by both men and women in this period, although the latter were paid a lot less than their male colleagues. In 1870, women in this occupation were paid on average £58 a year, approximately £3,631 in today's money. Men were paid £94 (£5,886 today).

Despite this, it became increasingly common to find female teachers, and even female headteachers. Rosetta Elizabeth Smith moved down to Cowes from Chester to take up a position at Cowes Elementary in the 1910s, after spending time in her hometown as a teaching assistant. Cowes Elementary was a primary school, and Rosetta was its headteacher right up until her retirement in 1943. Teaching did not require a university education as it does today, and women like Rosetta were sometimes able to gain the relevant experience working in a school environment and progress through the system that way. University education in general was tricky business, and most women wouldn't expect to attain it. Those living on the Isle of Wight would need to travel to the mainland. The first university in the UK to allow women to gain a degree was the University of London in 1878, although it was a long while before others followed suit. Cambridge was the last in the country to grant women degrees, finally submitting to pressure in 1948. They had first voted on the matter back in 1897, and the male students had been so outraged by the very idea of women with Cambridge degrees that they practically rioted, setting off fireworks near female colleges on campus and burning effigies of female scholars. Sadly, their sentiment was one that many men shared; women were not supposed to attain a high-level of education and go on to pursue well-paid career paths – they were supposed to stay at home to be wives and mothers.

Portsmouth Municipal College was just a quick trip across the Solent. Opening in 1908, it offered both day and evening classes, and allowed both men and women to attend.

Portsmouth Teacher Training College was originally all-female when it opened in 1907, and remained dominated by women throughout the entirety of its existence. The earliest available admissions register for the Training College dates back to 1911, and features one woman from the Island: Winifred Emma Williams, aged 20, who gave her address as Newport Road in West Cowes. She went on to use her qualification to pursue work as a teacher at Whippingham Elementary. The two organisations went through several different incarnations with several different names, eventually being granted university status in 1992 and becoming Portsmouth University.

Note how both Rosetta and Winifred were young and unmarried when they went into teaching. A marriage bar was in place in the teaching profession, meaning that authorities had the power to fire a woman from her position if she got married and refused to resign. This ban was not lifted until 1944. Many women got around this rule by marrying in secret and living in a separate house to their husband, or by entertaining a very long engagement. Rosetta might have actually taken this latter option; a newspaper report from 1931 reported the death of her fiancé, Mr William Slater, 'with whom she had been on the closest terms of friendship for many years'. Their marriage was only six weeks away when William had the seizure which led to his death, and Rosetta had reportedly handed in her resignation from teaching not long before. She seems to have been able to take this back though and continued to teach until her retirement seven years later.

Children were also taught a great many skills that would help them find employment outside of the education sector. As well as literacy and arithmetic, girls would be taught housewifery, needlework, and cookery. Boys were taught the more specialised subjects like carpentry, which were considered unsuitable for women.

In terms of where a child could go, parents had options – far more so towards the end of our period than at the beginning. For wealthier residents, there were grammar schools. Upper Chine Girls' School was a boarding and grammar school established in 1914, merging with Ryde Grammar School for boys in 1994. The old building has since been turned into holiday homes.

The fees for schools of this sort were far more than the average family could hope to set aside and, as a result, schools like this were set aside for 'posh' girls. The fee when Upper Chine opened was reportedly £100 per annum (£5,899 today approx.). That said, the daughters of military and naval officers 'received greatly reduced fees' according to several 1915 editions of the *Army and Navy Gazette*.

Lessons on the curriculum included English, modern languages, drawing, painting, music, cycling, and riding. This was extremely out-of-touch with your average school, where lessons in horse-riding were completely irrelevant; though many would have had horses, they would have been working animals. The sort of riding taught at schools like Upper Chine would likely have been more for show or competitions.

Dame schools were another popular choice for wealthy parents with little girls to educate. Run by women in their own homes, class sizes were small, and there was often a chance for students to board at the school for an additional fee. We touch on one of the more famous dame schools on the Island at the end of this chapter.

Then we had mainstream schooling, which was where the majority of the Island's children found themselves. This was closely linked with the local church, particularly in more rural communities, such as those on the west of the Island. Children would be expected to learn hymns and pray each morning as part of their school routine, and any children raised in families with a faith other than Christianity would likely have just had to go along with it for the sake of an education. These children would have been in the minority on the Isle of Wight, but they would have existed.

Mainstream schools were often co-education, meaning girls and boys were taught together in mixed classes. However, many chose to have them use separate playgrounds when break-time came around, for fear that boys were a bit 'rougher' when at play than girls.

For the more wealthy residents of the Island, there was also the option of a home education. This was usually done by hiring the services of a governess. Many Island celebrities were subject to this form of learning; famous photographer Julia Margaret Cameron would have had a governess whilst growing up in India, as would her children. A governess would have taught more subjects in addition to the arithmetic and literacy that other children were learning at public school, such as foreign languages (French was popular), and music.

Some children couldn't attend school due to physical reasons, such as Mary Gleed Tuttiett. Mary grew up in Newport, but suffered from a series of joint problems as well as severe asthma. Her father, Dr Frank Bampfylde Tuttiett, was one of the few medical professionals operating on the Isle of Wight in the mid-to-late 1800s. Through the income he earned, he was able to provide his daughter with a private tutor at their home on Pyle Street so that she wouldn't have to struggle through a public school experience. Mary was incredibly lucky to be in such a position, and she seems to have been aware of this; as an adult, she was a strong campaigner for the rights of her fellow women, both upper class and otherwise.

## Elizabeth and Ellen Sewell

Elizabeth Missing Sewell was born on Newport High Street on the 19 February 1815. 'Missing', a rather odd choice in middle name, is said to have been her godmother's surname.

Elizabeth had eight brothers and three sisters, all of whom were fortunate enough to be granted an education. Their father held a range of positions, all of which were well paid. The Sewells also had two holiday destinations of choice on the Island; a rustic cottage on St Catherine's Down called the Hermitage, and a parsonage in Binstead where an uncle named Edward resided.

The latter held a particular significance to the young girls because it contained a 'choice little library'. The majority of the books it contained were considered unsuitable for women and for children, and so the little Sewells were not to touch them without express permission. Still, they were enchanted by it.

Elizabeth and her older sister, Ellen, were sent to a boarding school in Bath when they were aged 13 and 15. However, their time there was cut short when they were asked to return home and handle the education of their younger sisters, Janetta and Emma – possibly due to Janetta's weak immune system. Elizabeth wrote in her autobiography that her 'whole heart was bent … upon teaching Emma and Janetta, and making them happy.'

Ellen used her new-found leisure time to attend parties and other social events, while Elizabeth continued to study under her own terms. Even so, the two eldest Sewell sisters remained close as could be.

By the late 1840s, the siblings were living with an aunt following the deaths of both parents, and Ellen and Elizabeth had taken up charity work within their local parish. Bonchurch's church, originally built during the Saxon era, was far too small for the size of its current congregation, and there was no local school.

Elizabeth was by this time writing and selling stories, all with a moral, Christian twist. When St Boniface's Church was completed in 1848, £10 worth of its furnishings (around £800 in today's money) were purchased with the profits from four of Elizabeth's short stories.

Her next project was to build a school, as the only education available for children in Bonchurch was a Sunday school run by a woman named Rosa White in her home. Elizabeth did this with her sister, who was an artist. Ellen drew six sketches and Elizabeth, along with five friends, wrote stories to accompany them. The proceeds from the sales of this anthology, entitled *The Sketches*, then went towards building the new school. A.C. Swinburne's father generously donated the remainder of the money needed for the project, although Elizabeth did later state that she thought they had managed to raise about £200 (around £16,000 today). Bonchurch National School (so named because it was endorsed by the Church of England's National Society for Promoting Religious Education) opened in the late 1840s/early 1850s. This school would likely have been aimed at educating the poorer children of Bonchurch, who were cut off from the facilities available in more populated areas of the Island during this time.

As well as helping to fund the education of the local children, Elizabeth and Ellen began to take a small group of children into their family home for lessons. They started with six local girls, including their own nieces (their brother had been recently widowed), and grew from there – seven was the standard number, although this could vary slightly. Defying traditional views on the education of girls, Elizabeth encouraged her pupils to read widely, and to question the world around them. The sisters always viewed their enterprise as a 'family home' more than as a strict school environment.

By 1866, Elizabeth was convinced that the middle-class girls of Ventnor (and the surrounding areas) needed a better source of education, too. She founded St Boniface School, which came to be known later as St Boniface Diocesan School. Exclusively for girls, St Boniface was run by Elizabeth, Emma, and Ellen, with a few sought-after places for well-to-do girls, some travelling across oceans even to be granted this privilege – Elizabeth Chanler, for example, was sent by her father from America. Word seems to have travelled, largely due to Elizabeth Sewell's successes as a writer. Her first novel, *Amy Herbert*, proved popular in the United States as well as at home in the UK. The school building still exists today, and while it is no longer used as an educational facility, a plaque on the front of the building does commemorate its original purpose.

After the death of her sister in 1897, Elizabeth's mental health began to decline and she fell into a deep depression. She outlived all of her siblings, Ellen passing in 1905, although their children – her nieces and nephews, as well as all the pupils she'd helped access an education over the years, provided for and took care of her until her death in August 1906. There is a memorial plaque for Elizabeth, Ellen, and Emma in St Boniface Church in Bonchurch, as well as a prayer desk 'given by friends in gratitude for her life and teaching' in 1911.

In a time when educating women formally was a controversial matter, the Sewell sisters went above and beyond to ensure that the girls in their community were given chances they were not receiving elsewhere – either on the Island, or in the UK as a whole. Evidently those pupils were grateful for these chances, as the memorials granted to the sisters throughout the parish are so loving and thoughtful, and they continued to look after Elizabeth as her mental health fell into decline later in life.

*The Dictionary of National Biography* speculates that her influence over young people was probably assisted greatly by her dry sense of humour.

# CHAPTER TWO

# Health

Prior the foundation of the NHS in 1948, healthcare as we know it today would have only been available to those who could afford it. This meant that a lot of women would have had to rely on an assortment of home remedies passed down from generation to generation.

Nowadays, many people view such traditional remedies as completely useless; and true, a lot of them are. However, we've also found through modern science that many of them might actually have helped, too. Lavender, for example, which has been used for centuries to keep bedding and laundry fresh and clean, has been found to have anti-bacterial, anti-fungal and anti-viral properties.

## Childbirth, and Female Reproductive Rights

In a world where women were expected to bear children, complications in childbirth led a lot of them to an early grave. A vague term, 'complications', could mean many things. The theory that germs caused illness, and that medical professionals should wash their hands before working with a new patient, was still in its infancy in the 1850s. Therefore many women died of infections that would have been easily preventable by today's standards, as well as of blood loss, or eclampsia.

For most women at the start of our time period, it was preferable to give birth in the comfort of one's own home rather than paying to give birth in a hospital. Often a midwife would be called, or perhaps a doctor – who would almost certainly have been a man, as the first woman (Elizabeth Garrett Anderson) didn't receive her medical degree until 1865, and this was an incredibly scandalous situation, not to become commonplace for several more decades thereafter.

The midwife for the area around Alverstone and Sandown in the early 1900s was a woman named Jane Bull, who had several children of her own as well; and another midwife, Edith Player, was working in the Ryde area at the same time into her seventies!

We can see from the business directories for the county that there were several women working as midwives throughout the 1900s, both married (like Mrs Rose Snow, who was working as a certified midwife on the Island in 1927) and single (like Miss Margaret Anderson, who was active around the same time). This was a respectable position for them to use as a means to make their own money, regardless of whether or not they had a husband. From 1902 onwards, an Act of Parliament entitled The Midwives Act made it illegal for an uncertified and untrained woman to work as a midwife. Midwives who were certified but lacked formal, supervised training were not banned outright, but they were gradually faded out of commission from this point on.

That said, in rural communities like the villages West Wight, outlawed midwives might have still continued to find business post-1902. It wasn't practical or convenient for someone way out on the coast to send for a certified midwife in Newport or Ryde, which would have had the densest populations of qualified midwives, being the main town areas of the Island. This, combined with a sense of loyalty towards the women who might have delivered your children prior to 1902, meant that many women continued to avoid the certified professionals.

The 1902 Midwives Act didn't affect the Isle of Wight until April 1903, when a warning was posted in *The County Press*. This explained that women had a further two years to claim the status of certified midwife, although they would need to provide one of several listed pieces of evidence in order to do so. These were either official certificates in midwifery from either The Royal College of Physicians of Ireland, The Obstetrical Society of London, The Coombe Lying-In Hospital and Guinness' Dispensary, or The Rotunda Hospital for the Relief of the Poor Lying-In Women of Dublin. A certificate from any other official midwifery organisation would need to be checked by the Central Midwives' Board. In addition to this, it was possible to gain an official midwifery certificate if a woman could 'produce evidence satisfactory to the Board' that when the Act was passed, she'd spent 'at least one year in bona-fide practice as a Midwife and that she [bore] a good character'. Any women wishing to continue their career in midwifery were expected to write to the District Council expressing their desire to do so, and would henceforth be expected to do so annually until she gave up her career or retired. Fines up to £5 were given to anyone found in breach of these new laws (around £390 today).

Some women, rather than consulting any sort of professional, went one step further and chose to have their baby delivered by a neighbour or a family friend. We know that women such as the Island's Alice Fuller, who would later go on to train as a nurse during the Second World War, delivered babies. She was known to be particularly unsympathetic to the agony of the mother-to-be, reminding her that 'it didn't hurt when it went in, now, did it?' Although the 1902 Act forbade this, it was legal for an uncertified 'midwife' to deliver babies if a qualified professional (either a fellow midwife or a doctor) was present in the room.

On average, for every 100,000 live births in the UK in 1850, 548 mothers died. Childbed fever was one of the most common complications. The introduction of antibiotics to the UK public in the 1930s contributed directly to a fall in serious cases of this though, and maternal mortality has been on the decline since 1934, when it was at 464.2 deaths per 100,000 live births.

At the end of our period in 1950, maternal mortality had fallen all the way down to 91.4 deaths per 100,000 live births. Mercifully, it is still declining rapidly; only nine deaths per 100,000 live births were recorded in the UK in 2015.

## Contraception

As long as there has been a risk of unwanted pregnancy, humanity has sought to prevent it from occurring. For women especially, sex came with a certain stigma. A baby born out of wedlock was infallible proof of her promiscuity, which would go on to affect every aspect of her life: the way others treated her, her relationship with family and friends, her job prospects – even her chances of finding a suitable marriage match could be negatively affected, as many men would not have wanted to raise another man's child.

Although the contraceptive pill was only legalised in the UK in 1967, seventeen years later than the end of our focus period, there were ways and means in place long before that to achieve similar ends. Perhaps the most unchanged of all contraceptive methods is the condom.

There is evidence that condoms were being made and used for the prevention of pregnancy and disease in ancient times; the Egyptians reportedly believed a linen sheath was a suitable way of preventing sexually transmitted diseases.

Animal materials were a relatively cheap, widespread resource used to create condoms throughout various different cultures. The Romans reportedly used goats' bladders, while there are stories from China of condoms made from lambs' intestines. Animal intestines were among the most popular forms of condom available to the European population in the 1600s.

It was around this time that the church stepped in, deeming contraception of all kinds – including condoms – immoral. Their fear was that it would encourage the masses to be licentious, sleeping around with several different people without needing to worry about any repercussions. Indeed, condoms had already been scientifically proven to prevent both disease and pregnancy; a scientist in Italy called Gabrielle Fallopius successfully proved that a linen condom soaked in chemicals could be used to prevent the spread of syphilis (which was one of the biggest STDs of the time), back in the 1500s, and an English report from 1666 credits 'condoms' with a decrease in birth rate.

By the time we reach the 1800s, there are strong sentimentalities about the use of condoms on either side. Concerns seem to have changed little over the last 300 years; people were worried it would encourage immoral behaviour or infidelity, or that there was not enough evidence that they could reliably prevent disease. On the flipside, others were fierce supporters of the idea.

Despite the opposition, the condom market was expanding. The first rubber condom was produced in 1855. These condoms were affordable and reusable, and made contraception more widely available among the working class. Condoms made out of animal skin continued to be popular, however, as these were even cheaper still.

In 1918, it was decided that condoms should be sold as preventative measures for the spread of disease, and not as a form of contraception. The result was an increase in sales in the 1920s, helped further by the invention of latex condoms. These could be mass produced cheaply, and sold at a low price.

Another method that we use today, but that has been practiced in some form or another for thousands of years, is the cervical cap. Although there were several different objects used for this purpose (have a look around you, be creative, you'll get the idea), the most popular were sponges and fruit peels. Today, sponges soaked in spermicide are available to purchase in many countries. These not only create a barrier for the sperm to try crossing, but the chemicals in the sponge ensure that sperm dies before it can make it anywhere near the egg.

It was during our period that vaginal caps were first commercialised, with them being introduced to the public in the 1880s. This was a huge step in allowing women to take control of their own sex lives.

Prior to this, the most common method appears to have been the use of a lemon. This has been traced back hundreds of years, and involves cutting a lemon in half and scraping out the insides. The hollowed out half-peel is then inserted into the vagina, where it acts in the same way as a modern-day cap; creating a barrier between the cervix and the sperm. Modern studies have also shown that the acidic nature of the lemon might actually have worked as a spermicide, increasing its reliability. There was, however, the risk of traces of lemon juice, which would irritate such sensitive tissue.

Of course, no method is 100 per cent reliable: bar one, that is. Celibacy has been a method of contraception ever since our earliest ancestors first realised that sex led to babies. Endorsed by the Catholic Church even today, simply abstaining from having sex – or planning it around your monthly cycle so that you only did the deed when at your least fertile – was seen by many as the only moral way of preventing a pregnancy.

Alas, there are complications. Celibacy in a traditional household, where the husband was in charge and his wife was expected to obey him, would have required both parties to agree to commit to it. If the husband wanted to live a celibate life and his wife did not, there were various means and ways of her keeping herself satisfied should she so desire. But if it was the other way around – as it often was, because childbirth was painful and scary and it was the wife who would have had to endure it – then there were probably many cases of the wife's wishes being ignored. Marital rape was only dubbed a crime in the UK in 1991. Prior to this, a husband could force himself on his wife without any repercussions – legal ones, that is. If she fell pregnant because of his advances, there was every chance that they'd wind up with another mouth to feed, as well as that he might lose her altogether; childbirth was, after all, one of the biggest killers of women at the start of our time period.

Interestingly, the majority of advertisements I can find for the Island in our time period are aimed at contraception for men, or cures for men's sexually transmitted diseases should the preventative measures fail. An 1858 edition of the *Isle of Wight Mercury* advertises a product called Triesmar I, II, and III 'prepared in the form of a lozenge, devoid of taste or smell.' The only indication we have that this product was available to women are the words 'adapted for both sexes'. Triesmar I was for spermatorrhea (involuntary ejaculation – often linked to masturbation at this period in time) and 'relaxation', and the advert claims that it 'restored bodily and sexual vigour'. Its users were 'now in the enjoyment of health and the Functions of Manhood'.

Triesmar II was for the treatment of gonorrhoea, and Triesmar III was 'a remedy for syphilis and secondary symptoms'. Both of these are sexually transmitted diseases that can affect women, and this was a cure that many may have turned to. The description of Triesmar III actually reads like a modern-day 'detox' advert: 'It searches out and purifies the diseased humours in the blood ... expelling ... all corruptions from the vital system'. It also supposedly cured scurvy and scrofula; two completely unrelated diseases – scurvy was caused by a deficiency of vitamin C, and scrofula was probably a form of tuberculosis.

## Abortion

No matter how dangerous and painful it was to bring a child into the world, the chances of surviving an abortion were far worse. As already mentioned, abortion was only legalised in the UK in 1967, so throughout our time period it was a criminal offence to have one, or to offer this service to others.

Having a baby out of wedlock could quite literally ruin a girl's life. The church liked for men to come forward about having children with women outside of marriage, and to pay a little money to help support their family over the next few years. However, it could be difficult to trace a pregnancy back to a man without the DNA tests we have today, and many men never owned up to these things. They were able to simply continue going about their lives, whereas a pregnant woman could find her whole world falling apart around her. She would often be kicked out of her home or disowned by her family. She would be branded such names as 'slut' and 'whore' by fellow members of the community. It would be even harder for her to find a job to support herself and her child, as few places would be willing to tarnish their good name by hiring her; this, combined with the practicality of needing to be at home to care for the child, as well as out at work bringing in an income to sustain it.

Most references to charities or refuges set up to help 'fallen women' during our time period seem to refer to London charities, such as London City Mission. Support for women on the Island seems limited, although we know it existed; a servant in Ventnor named Alice Wyatt was sent home from her position in 1879 after she 'lost her character, and [took] to a life of profligacy'. She was called to court for being drunk and disorderly, and the police produced a letter from a Home for Fallen Women offering her a place. Alice seems to have been fortunate enough to have parents willing to take her back, however, and despite not wanting to see them 'as she had so disgraced herself', she eventually chose to return home to Worcester rather than the Home for Fallen Women.

We also know that fundraising events were held for charities such as the Waifs and Strays Society, which supported children whose mothers could no longer care for them – often because they were unmarried.

Most 'fallen women' on the Isle of Wight, however, would probably have ended up in the workhouse. There, their babies would be born in the safety of a hospital and then taken away from them, and they were expected to work all day in drab clothes on meagre meals.

The Isle of Wight House of Industry was located in Newport. According to a rulebook for the site released in 1797 (it's unlikely to have changed too much in fifty years or so), unmarried mothers were kept apart from the other inmates, wore a variation of the uniform to make them stand out among everyone else, and had their names entered into a 'black book'. They were excluded from eating 'solid meat' on meat days.

This lifestyle hardly appealed to most people. So, short of grabbing a man and marrying him before the baby bump began to show (which a lot of women did!), what else could you do but seek out a life-threatening operation?

There were several options available. Women were advised to take a scorching hot bath, which was not a very reliable method but lacked the grittiness of most of the others, thus making it an appealing idea to many. On the flipside, some women tried to freeze their pregnancy away, lying in snowdrifts or taking ice-baths and often making themselves seriously ill.

One of the more famous methods was to insert something (often a coat-hanger, bent out of shape, however anything long-ish and sharp could do the trick; there were cases of using knitting needles or hat pins for this) into the vagina and puncturing the amniotic sac. This would induce a miscarriage. This method was easy to get wrong, however. There were cases of the implement getting stuck, and many more besides of women bleeding to death, or catching an infection in the aftermath and dying from it.

Women would also be known to throw themselves down the stairs in an attempt to abort a pregnancy, or to punch themselves hard in the stomach repeatedly. Some would even get into fights in the explicit hope that they would receive multiple devastating blows to the abdomen and lose their baby.

There were also traditional herbal remedies, often passed down from mother to daughter, and even sometimes available from midwives. Some of these did not work at all. Some worked very well. Some actually involved taking very small amounts of poison, which could easily prove fatal to the woman if she accidentally ingested too much. There were also herbs that could force contractions early and bring about a miscarriage that way.

This was probably one of the safer methods available to women in our time period, although it was still incredibly risky. One would have to buy the remedy from a midwife that they trusted, or seek advice from someone reliable and make it themselves. They would have to be able to afford to purchase the remedy in the first place; or be knowledgeable enough to harvest the correct plant by hand. And, of course, ingesting mysterious substances always has its dangers.

Imagine how desperate these women must have been, to knowingly endanger their lives in such horrible ways.

We can't know how many women on the Isle of Wight died as a result of an abortion, as these things were not recorded. People did not advertise the fact that they offered such services, and women did not tell everybody they knew that they had attempted to have one. We can say, though, that a lot of women must have died. In most cases, in a lot of agony, too. Throwing oneself down the stairs might have resulted in a quick death – but it also might not have done.

Alternatively, many women chose to give birth and then dispose of their child. Some did this themselves; at the beginning of our time period, prior to advances in crime investigation techniques, there were ways that were almost undetectable. If performed soon after the birth, it was easy to pass a baby off as having died within minutes of coming into the world, or even as being dead before exiting the womb.

If she didn't manage to see that through for whatever reason – exhaustion post-childbirth, sentimentality, the presence of someone else in the room perhaps – then there was still opportunity. On 18 March 1908, a couple were walking on the beach near Appley, Ryde, when they stumbled upon 'what appeared to be a brown paper parcel'. Initially walking by, their curiosity got the better of them, and they returned to untie it. They immediately informed the police when, within the parcel, they found the body of a baby boy. Described as 'fully developed', he was 'wrapped in a small toilet cover and part of a muslin curtain'. Bundled up thusly, he'd been put in a pillowcase, and then wrapped in brown paper and tied up with string. 'A piece of tape' pulled tightly around the baby's neck led a coroner to rule his cause of death as strangulation.

While we cannot be sure if it was the baby's mother who left him like this, it is the sort of thing that desperate women were drawn to do. The piece of tape around his neck makes this seem like a deliberate act, not an accidental one. Whoever left him on Appley beach, they were probably hoping for the tide to take him away before he was found by anybody.

For women who could not stomach carrying something such as this out with their own hands, there were baby farmers. A baby farmer was someone – often a woman – who took in unwanted babies and promised to care for them in exchange for a sum of money. However, often she'd do no such thing. Many women discovered that it was more profitable for them to charge the mother a lump sum, and then kill off the baby. There was no way that the money would last and continue to support the child, after all, and not all desperate women were in a position to pay regular amounts towards the upkeep of a 'secret' child.

Many women who took in babies for money did care for them, and raise them in kind, loving homes. Some baby farmers did 'accidentally' neglect the children in their charge, whether because the money they'd been given had run out, or they had children of their own to care for in addition who – in their mind – took priority over this outsider they'd taken in. A very large proportion of these women, however, did not care for their wards. Many did kill the babies in their charge deliberately, and this needs to be acknowledged and talked about.

On the Isle of Wight, a woman named 'Annie Ward alias Quinn' was charged alongside a man named William Francis Quinn. Despite not being married, Annie had adopted William's surname. They took in a little boy, but once his mother stopped being able to pay for him, their treatment of him became appalling. The prosecution said that it was 'evidently their intention to get rid of' the child.

Thankfully, this story had a happy ending; the child, covered in bruises, was taken away from Annie and William and given a new home where he 'was greatly improved'. Annie was sentenced to a month's imprisonment; William, fourteen days' hard labour. These seem light by today's standards, but at least they were being charged; it wasn't too long before this that people could beat children in their care with little consequence.

By the end of the nineteenth century, baby farmers did have something of a reputation. A lot of mothers must have been aware that they were possibly consigning their babies to an early grave when they handed them over. But, alas, desperate times call for desperate measures; and as mentioned before, entire lives were ruined by illegitimate pregnancies.

Baby farmers were replaced by child nurses as we moved into the twentieth century, although the principle remained the same; a woman, often unmarried or widowed, would pay someone else to take care of her child. This started as an informal arrangement between two women, but went on to be regulated by the Board of Guardians. Under the 1908 Children's Act, child nurses and foster parents had to be registered with their local Board, and had to report any children in their care. They also had forty-eight hours to report the death of a child, or they would face prosecution.

This happened frequently, including on the Island. A widow named Nellie Wood was charged in 1921 'for failing to register a nursed child since deceased'. She was fined £2 (around £58 today).

Advertisements were printed in the *County Press* and other local Isle of Wight newspapers, both by women seeking children to nurse, or for nurses to care for their child. One ad from 1900 reads: 'NURSE child wanted by a respectable married woman'.

Thankfully, as a more formal system for foster care and adoption came into effect in the UK, mothers who either could not, or did not, wish to keep their babies had somewhere to put them where legal guidelines were in place to ensure that they ought to be safe, and loved, and given every opportunity to succeed in life.

## Professional Healthcare

At the time of writing, there are several different medical practices dotted about the place on the Isle of Wight. However, many of these appear to be quite modern establishments. Where would a woman go if she needed healthcare before 1950?

First things first, many doctors and midwives were available on call. They could be sent for. If a woman had an accident at home or fell ill, she could send somebody – a child, perhaps, or a kindly neighbour – to fetch a professional to check in on her. This would cost a pretty penny, but without doubt it also saved a lot of lives. We know that the doctors operating from Pyle Street in the 1800s offered this service. Dr Frank Tuttiett attended to a woman named Jennet Fuller (née Cooper) when she had a stroke that rendered her unconscious. She lived in Whippingham, and had five children as well as a devoted husband. It's not hard to imagine one of them rushing into the heart of Newport in search of a doctor.

In a world where the average number of children a woman would have was around six, all of whom could fall ill – plus herself, her husband, and any other relatives that might be living with them – it was not uncommon to live with parents, in-laws, siblings, etc., or to take on a lodger – she could be looking at some pretty hefty medical bills by the time the winter was out!

It is no surprise therefore that many women chose to take matters into their own hands. Some of these methods were a little odd by today's standards. It was common procedure to treat a headache by wrapping your child's head in brown packaging paper that had been soaked in vinegar, like in the nursery rhyme Jack and Jill. Others, however, we still use in the twenty-first century. Keeping with the vinegar theme, putting this kitchen essential on wasp stings was a practice that probably found its origins in the home of a mother with a child who liked to run around outside barefoot in the summer. In 1895, a 14-year-old Island girl called Elizabeth Glew tripped and dropped her lantern while going to fetch a glass of water at night, badly burning herself. Her mother, Jane, dressed her burns with linseed oil before both she and her husband hurried Elizabeth to the Royal Isle of Wight Infirmary and County Hospital; tragically, Elizabeth died of her injuries.

## Vaccinations and Preventative Measures

Vaccines weren't widely available in the form we are familiar with today until the 1920s. Prior to this, people were extremely sceptical of the entire concept, and there were still many cases of people (particularly young children, the elderly, or people who already had weakened immune systems for whatever reason) falling dreadfully ill after a vaccination, sometimes even dying from it.

The 1920s saw the release of vaccines to the general populace for whooping cough, diphtheria, tetanus, and tuberculosis. These were all incredibly deadly diseases, and had claimed a lot of lives both on the Isle of Wight and throughout the rest of the UK before this point. Although these early vaccines were not quite as polished as the ones we use today, for the most part they seemed to work, and far fewer people died from these diseases than even just ten years prior.

That said, they began to be introduced to the Island populace in the latter half of the nineteenth century. With the effectiveness of the cure still yet to reach its peak, the number of people against the idea were many. A lot of parents felt that they would rather their child face the risk of catching diseases like smallpox naturally, than have them be injected with a tamer version. There is a case in an edition from the *Isle of Wight Observer* dated 1885 where a man was taken to court for refusing to take his son to a vaccination appointment. Indeed, this was such a frequent occurrence that there were specially appointed 'vaccination officers' employed to chase these things up.

A letter in the edition following this one was sent from a supporter of the accused, Mr Finch. Signed only as 'AN OLD INHABITANT', they detail to the reader several cases of children being worse off as a result of being vaccinated, although the evidence provided is based mainly on hearsay: e.g. 'the child died, and the neighbours all said it was the vaccination that caused it'.

This was not an uncommon opinion. There are still people today who vehemently denounce vaccinating children, and interestingly enough, many of their reasons for doing so seem to be the same as those of parents over a hundred years ago, despite the great leaps of progress we have made in the medical sciences since then. Smallpox, for example, was announced officially eradicated right across the world in 1980. This was due to vaccinations. Prior to 1980, and throughout the entirety of our time period, smallpox was a deadly disease that tended to hit babies and small children the most critically. Survivors were left scarred and, in severe cases, blind.

Regarding preventative measures, perhaps the most important one to come into common practice during our time period is the understanding of how diseases are actually spread. Doctors at the start of our period would not have understood the importance of keeping a clean environment. Tools would not have been disinfected between patients, and medical professionals would not wash their hands. If you had to undergo surgery, surviving the operation itself was only half the battle; you'd also have to hope the surgeon's bloodstained apron and dirty tools hadn't given you a deadly infection. Many surgeons actually viewed a bloody apron as a status symbol.

It seems unthinkable now, but when a Hungarian man named Ignaz Semmelweiss discovered a connection between dirty hands and childbed fever in 1847 he was called a madman. His hypothesis, that male surgeons who went straight from autopsies to delivering babies brought a higher risk of passing the disease on to their patients than dedicated midwives, invoked rage among the medical community. Most did not want to consider the idea that they themselves might be responsible for the deaths of so many women. It was decades before Ignaz' work was given serious thought, by which time he'd already passed away.

# CHAPTER THREE

# Women at Work

Throughout our hundred-year time period, it was expected that a woman would marry, and that the main source of income in her household would come from her husband. Therefore, it can be difficult to find a woman who worked all her life, or who managed to maintain a stable career. Most jobs for women would have been viewed as temporary. Even in working-class families where it was necessary for both parents to work full-time jobs, the husband was typically 'the breadwinner'.

There would have been far fewer jobs available for a woman to choose from in the 1800s through to the early 1900s than her male counterparts, although there were exceptions to this, with women on the Island taking on traditionally masculine jobs even at the start of our period, gradually increasing in frequency as time went on. Sarah Maria Alford, for example, was a dairy farmer on Baalambs Farm in Wootton. She appears to have taken this position from her husband after his passing. In 1861, a widowed Sarah Attrill was running a 400-acre farm in Calbourne, with five men and three boys under her employment. Her granddaughter Eliza Moses acted as housekeeper. On the 1881 census, 62-year-old Amy King was a retired builder living with her son – a carpenter. It seems as though her husband had also been a carpenter when he was alive.

Blanche Coules Thornycroft followed in her father's footsteps as a marine engineer. As these were not skills that were often taught to girls at this time (Blanche was born in 1873), it's likely she was primarily self-taught, or learnt through an unofficial apprenticeship arrangement between herself and her father. A testing pond for scale models was built at the family home in Bembridge, designed to look like a typical garden pond. It was dubbed 'the Lily Pond'. Blanche helped to build and test scale models in the pond, ahead of their creation as fully fledged vessels, using wires to tow them along the water at a constant velocity. One of Blanche's responsibilities was to determine ways to improve the speed of a ship. Frustratingly, the Lily Pond's success relied greatly on the weather, and an indoor test tank was built in 1911.

Blanche was one of three women admitted into the Royal Institution of Naval Architects in 1919, following the usage of several of her family's ship designs throughout the First World War.

The jobs available to a woman also varied greatly depending on her financial situation and class. For the majority of women living on the Island, we'd be looking at traditionally working-class jobs; domestic service, farm workers, laundresses, seamstresses, etc. Positions such as that of a governess in an illustrious household required a decent education, and typically went to young middle-to-upper-class girls before they married (if they did at all). And across the class spectrum, a woman would usually be expected to come home and act as wife and mother to her family, no matter how exhausted she might've been.

## Domestic Service

Service was a career path which many working-class women on the Island did choose to go into. Depending on the size of the employer's wealth and estate, a woman might find herself the only staff member, working as a 'general servant' and doing any odd jobs wished of her; or she might be one of several servants, and fit into a more specified role e.g. 'cook', 'housemaid', 'kitchen maid'.

There was room for progression in service, and a few women chose it in favour of marriage, working their way through the ranks to become 'head cook' or 'lady's maid'. Many would have started service as a girl with the hope they'd leave when they married, only to... not marry. They'd reach a certain age and then decide to make the best of their circumstances and perhaps apply for a better position in another house.

Some of Queen Victoria's own servants at Osborne House were Island girls; an incredibly prestigious position, and one that would have been greatly sought after. Elizabeth Cooper, for example, was born in Cowes and is marked down as a domestic housemaid at Osborne on the 1901 census. Queen Victoria actually died just before this census was taken, but there was still a household to run and her family to entertain. Elizabeth would have been part of an army of housemaids whose job was to make Osborne House look neat, tidy and presentable at all times.

Most Island girls, regardless of where they worked, seem to have gone into service sometime in their teenage years, and left their positions when they married; usually in their early twenties, although sometimes slightly sooner, or perhaps later in life.

The expectation was that a woman would marry. This was supposed to be her goal, her endgame. And she could not care for her own children or keep her own house if she was busy being employed to see to somebody else's.

Some positions within a household were also viewed as acceptable for women coming from wealthier backgrounds.

While you'd never expect to see a respectable middle-class girl working in the kitchens, she might have taken on the role of governess, which combined the role of nanny (which could be, and often was, given to working-class women) with that of a tutor. Most working-class girls probably lacked the education required by a wealthy employer for the tuition of their own children, thus making them unsuitable for the role; it wasn't uncommon for children from well-to-do families to learn several different languages, to play instruments, and to be accomplished in high-society dance techniques. Your average Island Jane would know English fluently and that was it. The dances she was likely to know were not the sort taught in a formal setting back then, and if she knew how to play an instrument, she was lucky indeed.

## Drapery, Dressmaking, and Millinery

These three also appear to have been incredibly common occupations for women living on the Isle of Wight during our time period. Unlike domestic service, however, a woman would not have had to give this up altogether if she married and began having children.

Building on skills she would have been taught as a little girl, typically these women would operate by word of mouth (although some did advertise in local newspapers) and take in orders for clothing and hats. They would be able to work from home, and could pick and choose hours that suited them. This meant that if their families needed them, they would be able to pause in their work and see to the matter without causing a disturbance or upsetting their boss (for they were their boss!).

It was also an incredibly good career for women who were unmarried for whatever reason – widowed, or otherwise – for the reasons listed above.

However, things become trickier when it is revealed that some of the census takers used 'dressmaker' as a codeword for 'prostitute', which would draw upon the same useful practicalities that made being an actual dressmaker or milliner so attractive to a woman in need of her own income: the ability to work from home, to choose her own hours, to decide her own fees.

This is not to say that all dressmakers were prostitutes! Or, indeed, that all prostitutes were marked down as dressmakers on the censuses. But one must concur that there is a suspicious lack of women marked down as sex-workers on the Island; it seems likely that at least some dressmakers were making a different sort of living altogether. We cannot know who, though, because in using a codeword their anonymity has been preserved. And that, while rather frustrating from a research standpoint, is rather lovely. A career in sex-work was not the sort of thing most women paraded around; rather something kept secret, or talked about in hushed whispers. There was a great deal of stigma associated with such work – more than today, even – and women were ostracised for these things. I think many of those operating on the Island during our period would be pleased to know that their secret has been kept safe all these years.

## Assistants and Helpers

There are several cases on the Island of women who had husbands that worked for themselves; think farmers, shop owners, and hotel managers. It is not unusual to see these ladies marked on the census as 'assistant [husband's job title]'. Often for a wife this space was left unmarked, indicating the absence of an occupation. That the husband seeks her help in running his business, and is comfortable enough in doing so to tell a stranger and have it recorded in a government document, is probably testament to a strong marital relationship. Some examples include Rosella Anchor, who assisted in the running of her husband William's pub, The Princess Royal in Newport; and the Johnson family, which was headed by Alfred Johnson, a dairyman. His wife Emily and four of their children – including all three of their daughters – are marked down as 'assisting in business' on the 1911 census. Mabel Shepard Wetherall helped her husband William in his occupation as a licensed victualler – meaning he sold alcohol. They had two young daughters aged 3 years and 2 months respectively, and Mabel's younger sister lived with them to help with their care. Fanny Chick assisted in her husband's work as a butcher, along with their teenage sons. Annie Hunt helped with her husband's work as a painter and decorator.

And these are just a few of many examples!

Even more often than this (for it was not a rare occurrence), we probably find that there were women who fulfilled the same sorts of duties in assisting her husband with his business, but who were not recorded as such on the census. Many men might have considered it demeaning to admit publicly that their wives helped out a great deal behind the scenes; many women might not have felt comfortable sharing this detail either. The ideal was that she be a doting wife and mother, which did not involve helping her husband with work matters. There was this idea among society before women won the vote that suggested they were incapable of making decisions – and, absurd as it might sound today, many people genuinely believed it. To know that a woman was making business decisions may have been viewed as a bold statement by some.

We also have cases of married women (possibly widowed) doing jobs traditionally viewed as masculine. Going through the 1904 commercial directory, we find such ladies as Mrs Raddon, who was advertising her services as a plumber; or Mrs Lydia Wickenden, who was a builder. These careers would not build on skills that were traditionally taught to little girls, but it does go to show that even a little over a century ago, it was impossible to fit all women into convenient little boxes. Not all of us have the desire to be a seamstress, or a milliner, or a homemaker. And this has always been so.

## Lodging Houses, Apartments, and Boarding Houses

Although not technically a career, many women chose to rent out various spaces at their disposal. This could be anything, from a room to a whole house, and anything in between. Taking in a lodger would have been ideal for a woman with a room to spare – perhaps because her children had all flown the nest? – and the money provided would certainly have helped with the household upkeep. That said, many women rented out rooms within their house while they still had little ones running about the place. It certainly must have been very busy, with a lot of people coming and going at any one time, but many families chose to take in lodgers regardless. It might even have been beneficial; depending on the nature of the lodger and their relationship to the family, they may have been willing to help wrangle the children when they were not working.

As well as places to live, there was also an abundance of women running hotels, inns, and places to stay. The Isle of Wight was an incredibly popular holiday destination by the time the 1904 commercial directory was created, and all of those tourists were going to need somewhere warm and safe to spend the night. It was very enterprising of these ladies to take a slice of that tourism pie for themselves by providing a service that many people would surely need, especially during the summer months. Examples of such women include Ethel Elarid, proprietress of a hotel marked down as 22–24 Hope Road, Shanklin. Born Ethel Parsons, her parents ran a private hotel in Shanklin while she was growing up, and she is recorded as 'assisting with business', along with her two sisters under the occupational column on the 1911 census. By 1939, Ethel had married and been widowed and was still in the hotel business. Her younger sister, Winifred, was also helping out at 22–24 Hope Road, although she was marked down as 'incapacitated' in the occupational column. With no further details provided, we can't know what Winifred's disability was or how it impacted her daily life. Still, she had her sister's support, and she was helping to run their family's business in some capacity.

Also cashing in on this unique opportunity were confectioners, photographers, and women who owned or worked in the many various tea rooms, cafés, and restaurants found dotted about the Island. Holidaymakers will always, inevitably, want something to take home with them; a stick of rock for their sister, a photograph commemorating their day at the beach. And nobody wants to cook dinner when they're taking a well-earned break! Thus these women, too, were incredibly entrepreneurial, and would have benefited enormously during peak season.

An example here is Mrs Flora Carwardine, née Corke. The earliest record I can find for Flora, after her birth index record, is the 1861 census. She was 2 years old when this was taken, and staying in the Temper Hall Hotel in Newport with her mother Jemima Corke. Jemima is marked down as the sister of the head of the household – the hotel's owner, George Gosden. There are also two other little girls staying with her: Esther, Flora's older sister by four years, and Alice, her younger by two. Although Jemima is marked down as 'married', she is not living with a husband named Corke on this or any other subsequent censuses up until her death in 1882, despite clearly having several more children in that time. She does not appear to have a job.

By 1871, Jemima was running The Valiant Soldier, a pub on the High Street in Newport. She had married the pub's owner, a man named James Harris, and her daughters are all marked down as 'Harris Corke'. Alice is missing, possibly dead, but a 1-year-old named Theresa Harris Corke is marked down. This is quite an age gap, as the next oldest child would have been Flora, who was 13.

Four years later, Jemima is recorded in an Isle of Wight business directory as running The Valiant Soldier alone. In 1881, she's there sans husband, but with her two youngest children: Thirza (Theresa), and William Cooke, who was 6.

Flora disappears off the record until 1880, when she married Henry Carwardine. She would have been around 22. Although apparently missing from the 1881 census as far as I can see, Henry had whisked Flora away to Lambeth, London, by the time the 1891 record was taken. Prior to that, he was running The Valiant Soldier according to a business directory from 1885, before apparently passing it over to the Matthews family.

They had two sons named Augustus and Edwin, and Henry was running a new public house in the big city. And then … well, then we can assume the marriage went south. Flora moved back to the Isle of Wight with their younger son, Edwin, and on the 1901 census is working as a confectioner. She's still marked down as married, although Henry is nowhere to be found, and 18-year-old Edwin appears to be helping his mother out by working as an assistant to a local bootmaker. Beach holidays were popular by this time, so Flora would likely have reaped the advantages of running a sweet shop during the summer. The winter months, however, might've been harder to handle.

Confectionary doesn't seem to have been a lifestyle choice for Flora, but rather a necessity. She needed to make money so that she and her son could survive, with a roof over their heads and food in their bellies. As time passed, Edwin went on to become a 'licensed victualler', that is, someone who could legally sell alcohol to others. This following in the footsteps of Jemima Corke, his grandmother. By 1911, Edwin was running The Lamb, Newport, with his wife Elsie. Flora was living with them, unemployed, but no doubt happy to be of use where she could be. She still referred to herself as married. Henry Carwardine, however, had been calling himself single since at least 1901. Divorces were hard to come by. I think what we might have here is a case of a separated marriage, with Henry moving on quite quickly, but Flora unable to for whatever reason; whether sentimentality, or just the sheer practical nature of knowing how it looked to have a son yet no husband. Whatever the case, she made the best of it in the end.

## Business Owners

As well as the above establishments, there are plenty of examples throughout Island history of women who ran their own businesses considered more conventionally masculine in terms of their output. Muriel Beal, for example, was the proprietor of a grocery in 1939. She appears to have inherited this position from her father, Frederick Beal, who is marked down as a grocer on the 1911 census. What's interesting here is that Muriel actually had a younger brother, Reginald, who was only three years her junior. Typically one would expect the family business to be passed along to him. The only other record for Reginald that I can find on the Island is a marriage certificate dated 1938, to a lady named Francis Jarvis. For whatever reason, a conscious decision was made within the Beal family to have Muriel take over the running of the grocery. Interestingly, her mother is marked on the 1911 census as 'assisting in the business' under the occupational column. Clearly this was a family who were unafraid to admit that the women worked hard, too.

Mabel Nymphna Carrington from London seems to have taken up being a market gardener between 1911 and 1939, possibly following the death of her husband. By the time the nationwide 1939 register was taken, Mabel was retired and living comfortably in Valerian Cottage, on Tulse Hill in Ventnor. There were often cases of women taking up work once their husbands passed, simply because they had to make ends meet somehow.

## World Wars One and Two

War affected all aspects of life in Britain, including on the Island, and including those of women. Although they were not allowed to sign up and fight on the front lines, their whole world would still have been flipped upside-down.

Mothers would have had to deal with their sons going away; many never to come home. Wives would be without husbands; sisters without brothers. These were people they cared about, their friends, their loved ones.

And in their stead, they left jobs in need of doing.

There were already many jobs on the Island that women were doing before the men left, whether officially or otherwise. Jobs like farming, for example, were already done by quite a few women – far more men, but still, a significant number of women ran their own farms. This would have meant that when the time came for the men to leave for battle, food supply would have continued. Prior to the First World War we also have records of women running dairies, working as butchers and bakers, etc. More women would have been expected to step up and take on these roles while the men were away, but there would have been others available to teach them the skills necessary. A short post in a February 1919 edition of the *Isle of Wight Observer* tells the reader that, when asked, 5,421 Land Girls 'answered affirmatively the question whether they wish to remain in agriculture after their demobilisation'. This, versus 3,278 who replied in the negative. Taken just a few months after the end of the First World War, this result clearly demonstrates how many women actually enjoyed working these physical, traditionally masculine jobs. The article is actually incredibly optimistic about this result, going on to talk about how there were hopes of further training being put in place for the women who wished to continue with their agricultural work during peacetime. We can assume that the number of girls running farms, dairies, etc. only increased into the 1920s.

As well as the jobs that would have already existed on the Island in some capacity, the wars brought opportunities for new ones. Many women trained to become nurses, and then either travelled to the front lines, or stayed at home to help out in one of the many hospitals that sprung up about the place. Several grand houses, including Osborne House, were turned into convalescent homes for wounded soldiers during the First World War, and many Island women trained to work in them. A letter signed only 'V.A.D.' (which stood for Voluntary Aid Detachment, and referred to a group of civilians providing nursing for wounded soldiers, without pay) sent to the *Observer* in April 1916 says that 'It is a proud boast that according to our population the I.W. holds a record for providing V.A.D. hospitals'. And indeed, in both wars, there were many. This VAD was writing to the newspaper in response to a plea for help in setting up a medical unit associated with a group called the I.W. Volunteers. Specifically, they were searching for 'patriotic ex-St John Ambulance members and Red Cross Volunteers'. She counters this argument by pointing out that most patriotic members of Island society were already doing their bit for the war effort. And how on top of that, the many hospitals already in place on the Island would welcome additional aid. One gets the impression she felt this proposed medical unit was rather redundant.

Volunteer work will be touched upon in more detail later, in the *Leisure* chapter.

# CHAPTER FOUR

# Love and Relationships

It was expected during this time period that a woman would marry, and that she would do so at a young age – particularly by today's standards. It was common for girls to marry in their early twenties, although this was usually to men of a similar age. There were, of course, exceptions. Some women married later. Some women married more than once over the course of their lives. Sometimes there were greater age gaps than, say, ten years. But all of this is still much the same today.

Marriage in 1850 was an altogether different affair than the one we've grown accustomed to, however. It was, in essence, a contract. A woman was viewed as the property of her husband. Anything she owned became his. She was no longer fit to inherit, as everything would be passed along to him and (hopefully) to their children. This was not changed until 1870, when the Married Women's Property Act altered the law enabling women to inherit, and to maintain ownership of money that they had earned in their own right. This was replaced by the 1881 Married Women's Property Act, which allowed women to own and control property. This Act also forced the law to recognise a wife as a separate entity from her husband, not just one part of his being, but her own person, with her own belongings and wishes for them.

Even so, marriage remained important business, and not the sort of thing one would want to enter into with just anybody. Women, particularly near the start of our period, would have needed a husband they could trust – even more so than today, because, quite literally, she would be putting her life into his hands. Any property she had would become his in the eyes of the law. All she had was his to own. With a nice man, this may not have been too terrible. He might have allowed her to keep her own things, to earn her own living by means of one of those respectable careers already mentioned a chapter previously. But even the nicest man may not always be nice, and the right man for her when she was 19 may not be the right man when she's 65.

## Divorce

Divorce was almost impossible for the average married woman to obtain. It was an incredibly expensive affair, and cost more than a year's wages for the typical Victorian family. Even if a marriage became terribly unhappy, most couples were forced to just grin and bear it. This left a lot of women in horribly abusive relationships without any means of escape.

Additionally, while it was possible for a man to petition for a divorce on the grounds solely of his wife's adultery, a woman would have to prove her husband's guilt in this as well as in another matter. A man's infidelity was not enough by itself. Possibilities of grounds for divorce included extreme cruelty, bigamy, incest, and sodomy. This last one is typically associated with homosexual relations, but the act itself was considered immoral by the church and thus by law – be that between two men, or between a man and a woman. And while it was without a doubt used to condemn homosexual men most often, it did affect straight men with wives who did not enjoy it.

If it was a husband accusing his wife of adultery in pursuit of a divorce, he would need to be able to provide evidence that he had not at any point condoned her actions or assisted her in her affair in any way (e.g. by helping arrange meetings between the two, or knowingly turning a blind eye to such events).

In addition to all of this, the only place in the country where a divorce was able to be granted was at the High Court in London. This would have meant at the very least an overnight stay in the city for an Islander, possibly even longer. It would have been even more expense (travel, lodgings, food, etc.) on top of the already extortionate divorce proceedings. None of this was feasible for the majority of women living on the Isle of Wight, who would never have been able to save up the money required to get their cases considered.

Wives seeking to end a marriage were not put on equal footing to their husbands until 1923, when The Matrimonial Causes Act was passed, in part a response to the growing role women had managed to forge for themselves during and after the First World War. This Act meant that women were also able to petition for a divorce solely on the grounds of adultery, without having to cite evidence of cruelty, incest, or any of the other acts previously deemed necessary. A further Act passed in 1937 made it possible for a couple to divorce on the grounds of cruelty, desertion, or insanity, as well as adultery. Only one of these was needed for the request to be taken seriously.

While formal divorces were difficult to acquire, it wasn't all that odd for couples to split and live their lives separately – often with separate partners to the ones they had married. Although this was considered somewhat strange towards the beginning of our period, it did happen with increasing frequency as the years moved onwards.

The divorce laws we are familiar with today did not come into effect until the 1960s, and so would have been too late to concern the ladies featured in this book.

Custody of children in regard to successfully divorced couples was already on the right path by 1850. A prominent author, socialite, and social reformist by the name of Caroline Norton successfully divorced her husband in the 1830s. At this time, children were automatically placed under the care of their father in the event of a divorce, as it was presumed he'd been the one providing for their needs financially. Caroline wrote an emotional pamphlet, explaining the plight of mothers, to Parliament, leading directly to the 1839 Custody of Infants Act. This granted mothers the right to petition the court for custody of children under 7 years of age. This was later extended to 16 in 1873.

If an unhappily married couple were fortunate enough to be in a position where they were granted a divorce, many women seem to have fallen back on the support networks of their friends and family members. Constance Ada Stevens, for example, is living with her parents in Godshill on the 1911 census. She's marked as divorced and living with her daughter, also named Constance Stevens, and a French governess named Yvonne Boncault. Yvonne was 18, as was the younger Constance, though the specification of 'French' seems to indicate that she was especially hired to tutor her in her own native language.

The only other successfully divorced women on the 1911 census for the Isle of Wight are Annie Pike Scott, who was living with her daughter's family, two nurses, and two servants; Fanny Butter, who was living with her younger sister Eliza and her husband; and Blanche Lucretia

Manton, who also had two servants, and was kind enough to squeeze 'Divorced my husband more than 20 years ago', into the tiny census box where one was supposed to write 'married', 'single', 'widowed', or 'divorced'. Blanche was 65 years old and living 'on private means'. As you can see from the mere fact that three out of these four households had staff in some form or another, divorce was generally an expensive business, and the people who pursued it successfully usually had money to spare.

The only woman who shows up on a search for divorces on the 1901 census is Emily Miller, who appears to be living with her stepfather. Again, following the apparent trend of husbandless divorcees seeking assistance from family members and friends.

Looking through census records back as far as 1841, when they first began to be conducted on a national scale, there seems to be no compelling evidence of a divorce on the Isle of Wight prior to Emily's. Or, perhaps, to Blanche's, since she was so sweet as to tell us that she'd divorced her husband more than ten years before the 1901 census was taken.

That said, many women separated from their husbands and lived out the rest of their lives in a different household. If you recall Flora Carwardine, the confectioner from the *Occupations* chapter, she appears to have taken this option.

Separation was also offered as a solution at trials for domestic abuse. In 1905, Mary Jane Bull tried to have her husband prosecuted in Ryde for persistent cruelty towards her. Among other things, she said that he withheld food from her, struck her, and alleged that their youngest child wasn't his. Once he pushed her over a bath. A string of witnesses each said that they had 'never seen any impropriety on the part of the wife'.

Despite having several people come forward to say that Mary's wish for a divorce was justified, the case was dismissed with the suggestion that she and her husband come to 'some sort of agreement to live apart'. A divorce was not given.

## Courting

With that out of the way, all relationships have to start somewhere! And very, very rarely do they begin with a divorce! So, how would a woman have gone about courting the object of her affections during our time period?

Our modern view of how our Island ancestors went about falling in love and wooing each other is based very much on the traditions of the upper classes. Such courtship would have been present on the Island, which has always been an attractive destination for the elite but became a particular favourite when Queen Victoria decided to make her home there in 1845. Freshwater especially is now famous for the celebrities who once resided there; Julia Margaret Cameron, Alfred Lord Tennyson, May Prinsep, among many others.

Courtship among these people was steeped in tradition. If a lady felt attracted to a gentleman (or vice versa), it was considered highly inappropriate for her to just waltz over and let him know. Instead, she would need to find a mutual friend to introduce her to him formally.

Until marriage, a woman and a man would be unable to spend time together unaccompanied by a chaperone. It was important that a woman was seen as chaste on her wedding night, which was rather difficult to accomplish if everybody thought she'd been throwing her virtue around. The chaperone rule was in place to protect her and her reputation. That said, it surely must have irritated many of them, who would likely have wanted to spend time with the boy they liked without knowing somebody else was watching their every move.

Marriage between the upper and upper-middle classes was usually less about love and more about money or politics. It was often viewed as something of a business transaction, with fathers seeking to marry their daughters into rich, influential families, and trying to persuade the eligible bachelors of such with a hefty dowry. The expectation was that a good, well-suited couple would learn to love each other.

That said, there were many cases of rich people who married for love – including several on our very own Island! Mary Ryan worked as a maid for Julia Margaret Cameron (see *Arts* chapter), who found her begging on the streets of London at the tender age of 10. Mary was one of Julia's favourite models, as well as something of a personal project; playwright Henry Taylor found Mary taking lessons with Julia's sons at the Dimbola Lodge in Freshwater when he visited the family in 1861, and reportedly said that she was 'rather naughty'.

The story goes that one of Julia's photographs of Mary caught the attention of Henry Cotton, who worked with the Indian Civil Service for much of his life before becoming a Liberal MP in 1906. Henry was enamoured and bought any and all photographs of Mary that he could get his hands on. Already acquainted with Julia Cameron, whose father had also worked for the ICS, and who had spent much of her childhood in India, he visited her at the Dimbola Lodge, where she went about trying to set him up with her maid.

The scheme was ultimately successful, and Mary Ryan married Henry Cotton in Freshwater in 1867. This rags-to-riches story was certainly not the norm, but it was incredibly romantic, and that it took place on our very own Island makes it all the better.

For most girls of Mary's station, though, being swept up by a rich photographer and falling in love with a future politician was a distant dream. So, what was courtship like for working-class Islanders?

Firstly, it's unlikely most women would have had a chaperone. There wouldn't have been the resources available to squander on hiring somebody, and most of her family members would be busy living their own lives – working, looking after children (be they younger siblings or nieces, nephews etc.) and keeping house. That said, a girl's parents would still have expected to have the ultimate say in her dating affairs. If they disapproved of a suitor they would tell her so, and she would be expected to heed their wishes and cease all contact with him. They could forbid her from going out to see him. They could threaten to beat her if she disobeyed them; corporal punishment was still popular, and it was considered more than ordinary to smack one's children for misbehaving.

Even so, you can be sure that many girls and young women went behind their parents' back to kiss boys in secret. Such things have always been so.

If a couple made the decision to marry, the man would be expected to ask the permission of the woman's father. Even if they had been seeing each other for a while, and everybody had been expecting him to pop the question, it was still considered 'the done thing'. There are still some circles today where this tradition is maintained, although in the western world it is considered less about the father giving his daughter away to her future husband, and more to do with respect for her family and with formality.

As times progressed through our time period, the courting process became more and more similar to the one we are used to today. It became acceptable for a woman to approach a man and, as life expectancy increased and the pressure to have children at a young age wore off, to perhaps date a few men before settling down with 'The One'. A woman would usually still be expected to settle down with The One eventually, and to have babies, but because vaccines had been discovered for most deadly childhood diseases in the UK by 1950, people could afford to take things a little more slowly.

Due to travel being much more limited, it was still extremely likely that a woman would marry somebody who grew up maybe as far as the next village over, but rarely much further. Island girls were also lucky in that they had Portsmouth just a short jot across the Solent, which had been a busy port city for centuries. This might have brought in men to meet from further afield. Mostly, however, she could expect to marry someone from her own neck of the woods, simply because travel for pleasure was so difficult for the majority of people. Cars did not begin to become affordable for the masses until the 1930s, and while modern passenger aeroplanes were invented that same decade, it would take a couple more decades before they were considered accessible to your typical, working-class family. Even today, air travel is too expensive for a lot of families who deem money better placed elsewhere. This would have been even more commonplace prior to 1950.

Limitations aside though, women could expect to meet men in much the same ways they do today. There were the childhood sweethearts who married young and the couples who met at work (e.g., girls who went into service as teenagers and wound up meeting their future husband in the form of the handsome young footman, perhaps). There were couples who met when out dancing, or drinking, or just otherwise having a good time and there were women who were introduced to a man via a friend or family member.

Online dating might have been out of the picture, but there were still ways to talk to people without needing to meet in person. The personal advertisements in newspapers would have fluctuated in and out of popular usage throughout our period, although they appear to have been largely used in the search for employers and employees on the Isle of Wight.

As well as personal ads, writing letters was a common pastime. As well as writing to friends and family, women often signed up to pen-pal groups and clubs designed to match them up with somebody so that they could exchange letters. This really took off during the First World War, with many soldiers desperate to have someone to write home to, and many women eager to help out with the war effort in this unconventional way. Many lovers met through the exchanging of letters.

## Marriage

Views on marriage a hundred years ago were a little different than they are today.

A woman would be expected to marry – and would be expected to want to. Little girls were supposed to dream of being good wives and good mothers. Many did. Of course, there would have been others who did not. A lot of these children would have grown up to marry and become wives and mothers anyway, though.

It was considered extremely undesirable to be an unmarried woman of a certain age, particularly once the suffrage movement began to take hold. The press liked to portray suffragettes and suffragists alike as ugly, man-hating witches, who often felt spurned that they could not find a nice husband. Interestingly, many of the arguments against modern-day feminism have a similar tone to them.

Provided she was of a Christian faith, which the majority of women on the Island would have been at this time, a wife would have promised during her wedding ceremony to 'love, honour, and obey' her new husband. This last part is particularly important, as it emphasises the power imbalance in a typical traditional relationship. If your husband didn't approve of something, then you didn't do it. If he wanted something, you would give it. If he had an opinion, you would agree with it – even when you didn't.

This would have no doubt resulted in many forms of subtle rebellion, the sort that could easily go unnoticed and unpunished; such things as meeting up with one's girlfriends for tea once a week, and using the time to gossip and compare notes on their marital affairs.

These meetings would also have been the ideal place for women to swap ideas of what my own mother refers to as 'man-management' techniques. These were little ways of making life easier, often passed down through families from mother to daughter, between close friends, wife to wife and woman to woman. Things like chamomile tea being an effective way of making one's man get an early night – or whisky, or lavender-scented candles. Platonic relationships between women are often viewed as 'catty', two-faced and cruel; although this is often the case, particularly in young girls, most long-lasting friendships bring with them a sort of loyalty rarely found elsewhere. We see examples on the census of girls letting their friends or sisters live with them when they have nowhere else to turn; girls standing up for other girls, giving them advice, helping them find their way. Flora Carwardine, for example, knew that when she separated from her

*The view of the Carisbrooke village from the battlements of Carisbrooke Castle. (© Chloe Bryant)*

*A drawing by Paquet dating back to the 1860s. The hoop skirts are clearly visible. (Public domain image)*

*Sisters Edith and Elsie Toogood in their Sunday best. (© Pat Channon)*

*Freshwater Bay. (© Chloe Bryant)*

*A different view of Freshwater Bay. To the right of the image, the Albion Hotel is visible. The earliest part of the building dates back to the 1600s. (© Chloe Bryant)*

*An artists' interpretation of how a cottage in Freshwater might have looked in the early 1900s. (© J. A. Howes)*

A portrait of Isle of Wight photographer Julia Margaret Cameron, taken by her husband Henry Hershel Hay Cameron. Julia lived at the Dimbola Lodge in Freshwater, which has since been converted into a museum dedicated to her life and work. (Public domain image, Metropolitan Museum of Art)

A traditional washing mangle. Articles of wet clothing would be passed between the two rollers, which would then be spun by turning the wheel on the right. (Pixabay, Creative Commons License)

*An etching by John Wanamaker from an 1894 edition of Book News depicting Maxwell Gray. Maxwell Gray was the pen-name of Newport-born author Mary Gleed Tuttiett. (Public domain image, Wikimedia Commons)*

*A portrait of Mary Ryan, taken by Julia Margaret Cameron. Mary was one of Julia's servants and a favourite of her muses. She went on to marry Sir Henry Cotton, a member of the Indian Civil Service and future Liberal MP. (Public domain image, Metropolitan Museum of Art)*

*A portrait of May Prinsep, taken by Julia Margaret Cameron. May holidayed on the Isle of Wight growing up, and moved to Freshwater on a more permanent basis after marrying Hallam Tennyson- son of the renowned poet Alfred Lord Tennyson. (Public domain image, Metropolitan Museum of Art)*

*A modern photograph of Ryde Pier. Ryde Pier was built in the early 1800s, and the basic structure has remained the same ever since. It would have been present throughout the entirety of our time period. (© Chloe Bryant)*

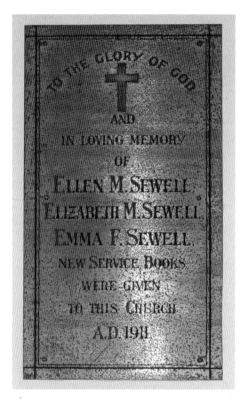

An image of the memorial plaque dedicated to sisters Ellen, Elizabeth, and Emma Sewell at St. Boniface Church in Bonchurch. (© Geoff Allan, Isle of Wight Family History Society)

This cartoon is a good depiction of the opinions many held towards suffragettes at the peak of the women's suffrage movement. The stereotype for a suffragette (much like it is for a modern-day feminist) was that she was physically "ugly" and bitter because she was unable to get a man. (© Getty Images, from the collection of Dr. Kenneth Florey)

husband and moved down south that her mother was living in Newport, and her sisters were no doubt nearby. May Toogood, when she moved to the mainland, went with her sister. And when suffragist Elizabeth Thompson was widowed, she knew that she could rely on her sister to take her in and give her somewhere to live. Marriage is a big step for anybody to take. Thankfully, most women throughout history would have been lucky enough to have a friend or a sister or a mother – somebody, at least – to hold their hand and help them through any rough patches.

Should a woman's husband pass away, she would have more than likely had to rely on assistance from family members or friends to see her through financially, too. A relationship where the husband was expected to bring in the bulk of the family's income meant an enormous loss in finances should he die unexpectedly; unless he'd served in the army, in which case women in the second half of our period could expect a widow's pension.

Some women were fortunate enough to have savings set aside for a rainy day such as this, but most would have had to rely on their parents or siblings for aid. Failing this, a widow would have found herself in the most dire of straits. The proportion of married women on the census records for the Isle of Wight House of Industry is by far dwarfed by the number who were unmarried or widowed.

## Same-sex Relationships

Marriage between two people of the same gender was only legalised in the UK in 2014. Sadly, this would have been too late for most of the women born during our time period as, even if a woman was born in 1950, she would have been 64 in 2014. While this isn't too late to get married, she would have spent most of her adult life unable to be with the woman she loved in the eyes of church and state.

Civil partnerships became available in the UK in 2005, when that same woman would have been 55. Legally these are similar to marriages, as they were introduced for same sex couples to experience the same rights, but some differences are apparent. For example, at the time of writing they have slightly different requirements in place for separations/divorces e.g. a marriage can be annulled if one half of the relationship was suffering from a transmittable form of a sexually transmitted disease at the time of the marriage, whereas this is not possible with a civil partnership.

Sex between two women has never actually been illegal in the UK, unlike sex between two men which was only decriminalised in 1967. It was generally frowned upon, and certainly considered unnatural, but it was never technically illegal. This makes it even more difficult to trace such women, as they could not be punished for their sexuality. At least, not in the traditional sense.

The fear of differing from the norm can be crippling, especially in rural communities. Lesbian and bisexual women would have likely faced severe prejudice if they tried to live their lives openly. They might have been refused jobs on account of their sexualities; they might have had abuse shouted at them in the street; they might have had to endure all this and worse. Families might disown a daughter, granddaughter, or sister if she openly preferred the company of other women. Unfortunately, this still happens today, but we are a long way away from where we were in 1950.

We find women on the census who never married, and we cannot know why. We cannot know if it was because they were uninterested in men or if they were just never able to find the right man. We find girls, unrelated, who live together, and we cannot know if they were just friends, or a lodger and her landlady, or if they were lovers. It's impossible, in almost every case, to tell.

Other options available to women besides a permanent lodger/landlady or domestic servant/employer arrangement were limited. Many women would have married a man simply because it was expected of them. They would have tried to fit into the mould society had created for them, and no-one would ever know that their affections lay elsewhere. This was probably the path most women chose.

Other options included seeking treatment for their 'illness', which coincides with the *Mental Health* chapter further on in the book. While homosexuality is by no means a mental illness, many people considered it to be throughout our time period. Concerned family members or frightened lesbian and bisexual women might have sought medical help for something they did not quite understand.

For religious women who felt uncomfortable with a heterosexual marriage, convents were a respectable way for them to escape that expectation without ostracising their loved ones. Their religion and sexuality would have been a great source of inner turmoil for a lot of these women, as the two conflicted. Many would have joined with the hope that a devotion to God and to their faith would help them get over their 'unnatural' feelings. While not all, or indeed even most, nuns chose their path for reasons to do with their sexuality, there were some.

Women seeking others of the same gender romantically have also historically made use of the indirect methods mentioned in the *Courting* sub-chapter; writing letters, personal ads in newspapers, etc. These were relatively safe ways of 'coming out', as it were, and exploring with some degree of anonymity. And while you'd never find an advertisement for 'Woman seeking woman' in the *County Press* during this time period, I'm assured that there were codes used to say just that. Tommy, for example, was used during the earlier part of our period to refer to a lesbian; the equivalent of Molly for men.

# CHAPTER FIVE

# In the Home

There is an old saying that a woman's place is in the home. Apparently, such a sentiment has been found to date back to at least ancient Greece. But how accurate is it really?

At the beginning of our period, most women would indeed have been 'in the home'. If they were working, it would most likely be in a 'domestic' job, such as a housemaid, a cook, or a seamstress. As mentioned in the *Occupations* chapter, many women would have also assisted in the running of their husbands' businesses or worked to keep them going should he have the misfortune to die first. While some poorer families had no choice other than to have both adults work, most normal working-class units living on the Island seem to have maintained a strict 'husband works, wife stays at home' code.

By the time we reached 1950, however, many women would have had jobs in their own right, doing things that would have traditionally been considered 'masculine'. The changing state of the world also opened a series of doors for women. Typing, for example, was a popular choice of employment for ladies. This would not have been possible a hundred years previously as the equipment needed to do it had yet to come into existence. Typewriters only came into wide usage in the 1880s, although once they'd made their mark they became a staple in most offices right up until the 1980s!

One thing that would have been present throughout our hundred years is the idea that men were supposed to be the main earners within a household. If a woman did go out to work, it was as a supplement to her husband's income. It was probably part-time, and she probably wasn't earning enough money to pay the bills. Often, her money would go towards buying treats, such as sweets for the children or cigarettes for herself and her man.

That said, one of the duties a wife might be expected to fulfil was financial management. She would take her husband's income and figure out what to put where, which bills to prioritise, how much to set aside for groceries, etc. etc. Upper-class wives might have been able to entrust these sorts of duties to a housekeeper. For the majority of families living on the Isle of Wight though, such a luxury was not a justifiable expense, and the task would be left to the woman of the house.

This was actually a general trend. The duties of an upper-class woman would vary drastically from those of your average housewife. She would have had a nanny to care for the children, a housemaid (or several) to handle the cleaning, and a cook to prepare meals for family and friends. A very rich woman might even have had a personal maid to help her get dressed in the mornings. But how would she spend her day, if it was not doing housework?

Well, charity work was popular. It was not uncommon to find rich women who were patronesses of charities. She would also have chance to explore and dedicate more time to some of the things mentioned later on in the *Leisure* and *Arts* chapters – painting, for example, was an acceptable hobby for women to pursue. As was singing, or learning a musical instrument such as the piano.

It is worth noting that most very rich women did have very large houses to run, and that these would have been difficult to keep clean all by oneself!

Most women, however, did not have homes the size of Osborne House or the Dimbola. Very poor women might only have had a single room to take care of. The majority of ladies, however, would have had a little house to look after. They (or their husband, or father) might not have owned the house; it may have been rented; but it was a roof over the heads of them and their families.

The typical weekday would begin with the woman waking up bright and early. If she was a stay-at-home wife, she would probably be expected to prepare breakfast – for herself, for her husband, and for their children. This could vary from household to household, however, and no doubt there were some husbands willing to fend for themselves if they awoke first.

Children would usually take themselves to school. Often the older ones would be entrusted with watching over their younger siblings. Once she had seen her family out of the door, she would have the day to herself – in a sense. She would be expected to do the household chores, but she would have the luxury of a few hours spent alone. These are the sorts of small pleasures most women cherish.

Housework would vary from day to day, and would have been far more arduous and time consuming at the start of our time period. After the Second World War, vacuum cleaners became affordable to most middle-class families, and have gradually increased in popularity to become the household staples they are today. A fortunate, well-off woman in 1950 might have had access to a washing machine as well. Dishwashers didn't come into domestic use until after 1950. No matter when during our hundred-year-long time period a woman was from, you can be sure that she would be elated if you showed her a modern kitchen. Dishes she didn't have to wash and dry by hand! A floor she didn't have to sweep with a brush on her hands and knees! Clothes that washed and maybe even dried themselves! This was the stuff of dreams, a crazy vision of the future that seemed unlikely to ever come true. If you're ever feeling down, imagine introducing your great-great-great-grandmother to a washing machine.

The lady of the house would be expected to buy the groceries. This would have been done by visiting a series of specialised shops – a butcher for meat, a greengrocer for fruit and vegetables, etc. – rather than doing it all in one place as we do today. The first supermarkets weren't introduced successfully to the UK until 1948, and they didn't cross the Solent until the 1960s.

The entire shopping experience would have been much different back then. Most of the shop's stock would be kept behind the counter, so rather than wandering around with a basket the customer would have gone straight to the person on duty and asked for what she wanted.

Even after the introduction of supermarkets to the Island, many women continued to shop in the traditional way. The Isle of Wight is lucky enough to still be somewhere it's possible to do this if you happen to be in one of the more rural areas. There's something to be said about an old-fashioned English sweet-shop, isn't there? Particularly one by the seaside.

As well as shopping, the woman of the house would be expected to keep everything clean and tidy. Before vacuum cleaners, this was mostly done with brooms, brushes, dusters and cleaning rags. While we do still use all of these today, we don't rely on them. Women in the 1800s/early 1900s would have had to, because they wouldn't have had anything else to use instead.

If she lived with any children too young to go to school, it would fall to the woman of the house to care for them. She'd prepare breakfast and lunch for them, and try her best to keep them entertained throughout the day. This, while also beating the carpets, cleaning the floor, wiping the surfaces, preparing any food for dinner that needed to be readied in advance, along with all the other things a woman was expected to do.

Laundry was typically given its own designated day of the week, and was much more intensive than it is today. Prior to the advent of domestic washing machines, clothes would be washed by hand in a bowl of soapy water using a scrubbing board. The excess water would then be squeezed out using a mangle. An item of clothing would be passed between the two rollers, which would spin as the handle on the side was turned, and force the clothing through to the other side. To get through the laundry of an entire family in this manner would have taken enormous physical strength, as mangles were tough. They were also dangerous enough to be the sort of household gadget some mothers would forbid their children from touching, as fingers could easily get caught between the rollers and crushed.

The mangled washing would then be hung up to dry on a line – outdoors if possible, indoors by the fire if not. It would then be ironed flat and folded ready to be put away. Electric irons did exist by the early 1900s, but they would not have been widespread on the Island until much later. Instead the majority of women would have used the more traditional variant, which was made of cast-iron (hence 'iron') and left to warm by the fireplace. She would usually have two or three, and switch the one she was using when it cooled for the one already by the fire so that she could continue her work without pause.

Depending on what her husband did during the day, he would most likely be home some time after dark, particularly in the winter months. He would probably expect dinner to be ready for him, or almost ready. He would tell his wife all about his day at work, and she would be expected to listen and be interested – or at the very least to convincingly feign interest. Society dictated that a man's day was more exciting, and more important, than his wife's. Many women probably wouldn't have seen fit to regale him with tales of their recent exploits, and often those who did would find that their men stopped listening. This was to be forgiven, because he had had a busy, stressful day. The home was meant to be a place for him to relax. Society did not often acknowledge how busy and stressful life can be for the average housewife, for whom the home was somewhere to be proud of, to keep clean and safe, and well stocked with food, clothes, and all those little elixirs mothers keep in the bathroom cabinet. Where was she supposed to relax?

Most women, even today, will admit to hiding in the toilet at least once when they needed a little peace and quiet. But no matter how determined she may be, even the most stressed stay-at-home mother and housewife cannot stay in the bathroom forever. So where could she go to unwind?

# CHAPTER SIX

# Leisure

A woman's place may have been thought to be in the home, but she would be expected to leave it all the same. The ideal woman was not a hermit, nor was she a well-versed traveller.

She was somebody who more than likely went out a few times a week to unwind.

Many of the Island's most beloved tourist attractions began to develop during our time period. Blackgang Chine was bought by Alexander Dabell in 1842, and remains in the care of his descendants to this day. Regarded by many Islanders as Britain's first theme park, Blackgang was named for the local legends of smugglers hiding their treasure in the cliffs below it. Generations of children have been enchanted by the dinosaurs, pirates, and fairies found within.

It would have been a very different place 150 years ago, however, with the ravine (or 'chine') in its name still intact. Pathways were built down to it, and romantic Victorian gardens filled the remainder of the space. The Chine Café would also have been present, originally built as a hotel by the man who owned the site before Alexander purchased it. The puppets and models it is renowned for, however, were not introduced until the 1960s and 70s.

Osborne House, beloved holiday home of Queen Victoria, was first opened to the public in 1904 – although only the ground floor was accessible. Prior to this, the palace was used as a retreat for the queen and her family. Complete with a private beach, a cottage for the children to play in and practise their homemaking skills, and a vegetable garden for them to learn how to grow their own produce, Osborne truly was an escape for the royal family.

Most of the rest of the grounds were used as a convalescent home for officers, or as a naval college. This did not cease until 1933, when a series of private tenants went in and out of its doors. Queen Elizabeth II gave permission for Queen Victoria and Prince Albert's private rooms to be opened to the public in 1954, and more and more of the house has been revealed as time has progressed, with English Heritage taking ownership of the site in 1986. The most recent addition (or re-addition) to the site at the time of writing is the Swiss Cottage, which was opened in 2014, along with an exhibition on the lives of the royal children.

But while many Islanders would have taken pride in these more notable attractions (and still do to this day), they probably wouldn't have visited them all that much. It would have been something reserved for a day trip in the summer, perhaps, not somewhere they went every week.

Where they did go would have depended a great deal on what they wanted to do. If a woman wished to eat out, which was always a pleasure as it meant a meal she'd not had to prepare and cook herself, then there were countless options! Many of them are still in operation today. The Old Thatch Teashop in Shanklin, for example, has been in use as a tearoom since around 1940. Even if not visiting for a full meal, tearooms were a convenient little place for

women to meet up with their friends and discuss things –
like recent events, and their home lives, and their dreams.

## Clubs and Societies

Some women preferred something a little more regimented;
something that happened at the same time every week,
in the same place, perhaps with fun little events thrown
in (like charity bake sales, or fossil-hunting trips on the
coast). This was where clubs and societies came in.

Groups such as these were usually gender-segregated –
for example, The Women's Institute (WI), as the name
suggests, was exclusive to women. This would have
made them a safe place for ladies to learn new skills and
make friends, without the restrictions that might've been
imposed by a husband or father.

The first two branches of the WI on the Isle of Wight
were established on the same day in the May of 1919:
Ningwood and Shalfleet, and Wooton Bridge. The latter
has since been suspended, although Ningwood and
Shalfleet is still running today.

For younger girls, the Girl Guides were already
established on the Island by the 1920s, and the Girls'
Friendly Society also had a strong local presence. This
latter group was established in 1875 and run almost
entirely by women, which was remarkable in an age when
most people didn't trust women to run anything at all.
Queen Victoria herself was the organisation's patron.
While the children attending these groups would not have
been old enough to be escaping husbands and housewifely
duties for the evening, they would have enjoyed this chance
to be little girls, among other little girls, having fun and
learning new things. In the July of 1894, the Brading,
Bembridge, St Helens and Sandown branches of the

GFS came together to organise a festival. Over seventy people attended. There was tea and games, and reportedly 'the sea-saw roundabout was in great request'; children, it would seem, haven't really changed. Mrs Summer, the branch secretary, gave premiums to Alice Baker, Fanny Wright, and Sarah James, for their help and support in running the groups.

The fact that the local branches of both the guides and the GFS would have been run and overseen by women is incredibly important. This would have provided those women with something outside of their homes to put energy and time into, and the little girls in their charge with a positive female role model to look up to. While most girls would have had a mother – whether their birth-mother or a stepmother – many others wouldn't. Mothers often died giving birth to younger siblings, or fell ill. And some mothers were just terrible, for there have always been abusive parents. For some girls, their guide leaders would have filled an important role in their lives that might otherwise have been left unattended.

## Charity Work

Charity work was an acceptable pastime for women of all stations to partake in. While working-class women may not have been able to donate money or resources in the way that their middle- and upper-class counterparts could, they could still donate their time and their abilities.

Many became involved in charity work through the clubs and societies mentioned above. The WI was founded during the First World War with the intention of giving women a place to make friends, learn new skills, and help their local communities. These values are still at the core of the federation today. The WI would have raised a lot of money for local charities through events like bake sales and raffles at fairs, just as they do there now. The guides and GFS, also, would hold similar such events and donate the proceeds to charity, too.

Schools would also do their bit for their community, often by putting on plays and donating the ticket sales, or by selling artwork and other products created by the children. A 1922 ballet performance by Upper Chine Girls' School raised funds for the Waifs and Strays Society, which supported the children of women who could no longer care for them – often those of unmarried mothers.

The First and Second World Wars brought with them new causes at which women could direct their aid. As well as raising money for troops at the front, ladies would get together to make or gather supplies to send too. During the Second World War, for example, a 'small knitting party' made up of Mrs Archibald Smith, Mrs Hilliam, Miss Fryer, Mrs Brading, and Miss Rosetta Smith knitted between them 421 articles for the Royal Artillery Comforts' Fund. These included 'pullovers, mufflers, socks, gloves, mittens and helmets'. There was a strong sense of community spirit created by both wars, increased greatly by the fact that everybody would have known somebody who was fighting. Even those who could not afford to spare money often would have donated their time and skills towards aiding Britain's troops.

In terms of donating one's time, many women chose to become volunteer nurses during the wars, often with a charitable organisation such as the Red Cross. They would have taken classes and been trained in medical procedure before being allowed anywhere near injured soldiers, and needed to complete three years of satisfactory service before they were permitted to wear the Red Cross badge.

On the Isle of Wight, there were ten military hospitals during the First World War; one in Freshwater, one in Ventnor, one in East Cowes, two in Newport, three in Ryde, and two additional ones reserved for officers only. During the Second World War, there were two Red Cross hospitals in operation on the Island, and several others unaffiliated with the charity, as well.

There were also little acts of time-giving that were much smaller in scale, although still greatly appreciated by the community. For example, Rosetta Smith was remembered in her obituary for her 'unfailing cheeriness and kindness of heart'. Much of her work was through her local church, St James's in East Cowes, where she polished the brass and trained the Sunday-school teachers (she was a teacher at a local school herself during the week).

That said, some people did not want to be helped by charity workers; and some charity workers were less than the kind, humble image they hoped to present. The Salvation Army in particular seems to have had a rough time in its early days on the Island, with reports of heckling in the street and rumours about its members using the money raised for their own gain. It's worth noting that the Salvation Army is an incredibly Christian charity, with traditionalist Christian views; not everybody would have agreed with its values, even over a hundred years ago. Not everybody on the Island was Christian for a start. Although it would have been the majority religion, there was also a strong Jewish community, and the Isle has always been a haven for pagans (although they may not have been particularly open about this back then).

Parts of Ryde and Newport were also, for lack of a better term, a bit rough in the late 1800s. You can imagine how it might have hurt someone's pride to be offered help from somebody in a better position financially than oneself, and you can imagine how they might have lashed out at them over such a preposition. Toxic masculinity meant that many men thought it was their duty to provide for their families, and it was an insult to be offered charitable help as it meant that they were failing in their roles as husbands and fathers.

In conclusion, despite its reputation as an easy little dalliance to keep sweet little women occupied, charity work brought with it hardships and dangers not always reported on. It was not for the faint of heart.

## Hitting the Town

The subtitle used here is a little misleading, as for the earlier part of our time period the only real 'town' on the Island was Newport. Ryde, the other hub of activity there today, started out as a little fishing village.

Still, there was much to do. More than strolling on the beach or drinking at the pub, which was typically considered a man's domain anyway, what could a girl do besides being helpful in her community?

Well, much like today, she could dance. She could put on a nice dress, paint her face with makeup, do her hair, and go out with her girlfriends. A lot of women met their future husbands this way.

Many hotels, village halls, and other public spaces could be rented out for a bit of a bash. There were also regular dances scheduled; a newspaper advert from 1919 talks of how Jacqueline Stevens from New York had 'organised a series of Dances' at the Pier Hotel in Seaview. These were held on Mondays, Wednesdays, Fridays, and Saturdays, 8pm – 11pm. Tickets cost 5 shillings each, and Jacqueline's jazz band appears to have been performing. She also offered private dance lessons 'in all the latest society ball room dances – Tango, American Jazz Reel, Shimmy Shake…' While classics today, these would have been incredibly new and exciting back then – like taking a pole class nowadays.

## Parties and Fêtes

Like any rural community, the citizens of the Isle of Wight have always been interested in a good party. In 1852, the *Isle of Wight Observer* talks of an annual fête held by Queen Victoria and Prince Albert in honour of the latter's birthday. Invitations to this were extended to 'the labourers and workspeople employed on the estate and their wives; also to the seamen and marines of the Royal yachts, the coast-guard and Trinity-house men, and the detachment of the 86th Regiment quartered at East Cowes'. Lunch was provided, and followed by country dancing and foot-races. *God Save the Queen* was played as the royal family took their seats, and when they retired.

Not all parties were held by the queen, although the basic itinerary of food, dance, and a live band would probably have remained the same. Looking through newspaper archives, there seems to have been a great love of 'pole dance' at such events; I suspect the journalists of the time were referring to a maypole with ribbons, and not our modern take. Country dancing and quadrilles also seem to have been incredibly popular.

## Magazines

Without social media to keep them up-to-date with events outside of their own community, or TVs packed with hundreds of channels to give women an idea of life elsewhere, magazines were a crucial part of many ladies' lives. They provided a window into the rest of the world, which would have been especially exciting to those born and raised in rural communities and who had experienced nothing else.

The earliest women's magazines were targeted towards upper-class women, who would have had the time to sit down and read them. This began to change with the introduction of publications such as *Englishwoman's Domestic Magazine* (first published in 1852). Edited and written initially by Samuel Beeton, many of the columns were later passed into the charge of his wife, Isabella. Interestingly, it is *Isabella* Beeton whose name is more well known nowadays; she found fame writing recipe and housekeeping books, many of which are still available for purchase today.

Magazines like the *Englishwoman's Domestic Magazine* talked about such things as housekeeping, pet care, relationship advice, and craft ideas. It also went on to incorporate a feature with a sketch of the latest fashion from Paris, and a pattern so that readers could attempt to whip up something similar at home. This went a long way in helping working-class women keep up with trends they otherwise would have had no way of ever being able to afford, as they could make faux versions of high-end products for a fraction of the retail price.

Magazines specifically aimed towards a younger readership did not come into print until later. *Peg's Paper*, one of the first, ran from 1919 to 1940. With instalments released weekly, this was in many ways a predecessor to the regular TV serials teenagers consume today. These were often romantic stories, with everyday girls being swept off of their feet by rich, handsome men. This was some of the first entertainment aimed specifically at young girls, and it *sold*. These were often also girls with jobs – shop-girls and farm-workers and apprentices – so they had money to spend on such frivolities, where before the First World War many working-class girls would not have done. Timing was key to *Peg's Paper*, and other such publications', success.

# CHAPTER SEVEN

# Fashion

One way of getting into the head of a woman from any given time period, is to get into her shoes; or at the very least, to understand what kind of shoes she was probably wearing on a day-to-day basis.

At the start of 1850, the fashion was incredibly impractical. This was the era of hoop-skirts – that is, a series of rings (often made from whalebone) worn beneath the skirt and paired with a corset to create a perfectly crafted silhouette. She'd likely wear several petticoats beneath her skirt to help make it seem bigger still.

For your average everyday woman, the above just wasn't sensible. Trying to clean the floor in a hoop-skirt and corset would have been practically impossible, for a start. Whether she went out to work or she stayed home and kept house, most women would have admired the fashion of the times from afar. They would have a couple of outfits which they wore in rotation and patched up as much as possible before discarding. They would also have one 'best' dress, reserved for church on Sundays and for special occasions.

Hoop-skirts began to fall out of high-society fashion in the mid-1860s, with emphasis shifting back; the trend became to enhance a woman's behind instead. Bustles were worn in place of the large crinolines favoured a decade earlier. The bustle continued to be popular for many decades thereafter, and was far more practical than its predecessor; a bustle was much easier to do the housework in, I would wager, than a giant crinoline hoop-skirt!

Fashion in the 1870s came with tighter skirts, featuring less of a train at the back. Princess Alexandra of Wales had shot to fame when she married Queen Victoria's eldest son in 1863, and her influence on fashion was profound. Alexandra wore choker necklaces and blouses with high necklines in order to hide a scar on her neck. These became adopted by the women of the UK.

Corsets that forced the body into an 'S' shape were popular through into the 1900s, thrusting the hips backwards and the chest forwards. The effect of this was sometimes enhanced by ruffles at the breast, creating the illusion that the area was fuller and more rounded.

Influences from other cultures were also drawn into wear among high-society women, with draped fabrics and vibrant colours enjoying attention in the UK for the first time.

The First World War had a profound effect on fashion around the world, as it did all aspects of life. Practicality became crucial as women were urged to do their part for the war effort, whether as nurses or in factories or on farms. By 1919, the coveted 'S' silhouette had been abandoned altogether, and dresses were far less constricting. The ideal was, on the flipside, to dial down the more 'womanly' parts of the body; that is, the breasts and the behind. A flat, almost column-like shape was the goal. In the 1920s, this progressed further still, with the waistline dropping down below the hips.

The 1930s saw influences drawn from the pre-war days once more, although never quite reaching the same heights of impracticality; a woman could easily be stylish and do her own housework in the 1930s. The bias-cut skirt became popular, which allowed the fabric to drape in a way that accentuated a woman's natural curves.

The Second World War influenced fashion yet again. 'Make do and mend' was a government slogan encouraging members of the public to make their clothes last as long as possible, because fabric was in short supply. There were no pleats in skirts, no trimmings around hemlines. As in all other aspects of life, women tried to find compromises. Unable to get their hands on nylon stockings, young women would often paint their legs in gravy before a night out, using an eyeliner pencil to draw faux seams up the backs, and pray that it didn't rain.

By the end of our period, women's fashion had changed so drastically that a woman from 1850 would probably be thoroughly confused by it. Rather than enormous hoop-skirts, it was pencil skirts that were popular: curve-hugging and tight. Full circle-skirts were also popular. These are not to be confused with hoop-skirts. Circle-skirts are usually around knee length, and flare out when the wearer spins round suddenly.

Floral patterns in clothing were popular; in 1850, these would have been much more expensive to manufacture.

As a general rule, things like fashion trends probably reached the Island a little later than they did the rest of the UK. Likely Victorian women holidaying on the Island in an attempt to mimic their queen would have found the clothing of most Islanders almost quaint. They'd venture out along Cowes beach with their long trains, and be fascinated by the local women they saw still wearing the bustles that London had favoured several years ago.

That said, women on the Island did have access to the fashion magazines that so influenced their changing culture, and many would have been more than capable of copying the designs provided within them if they had the time to do so. *The London and Paris Ladies' Magazine of Fashion*, for example, was available 'at all booksellers' in the early 1860s.

# CHAPTER EIGHT

# Art

Artists of all kinds – painters, poets, actors, authors, musicians, etc. – have flocked to the Isle of Wight for centuries. Something about the very nature of the place is poetic somehow, and people go there to create. Freshwater especially has a particular reputation for being where the artsy folk settled long ago, with remnants of their lives left over even now: Tennyson Down, the Dimbola Lodge, Farringford.

There have always been female artists, although, as in many other areas of history, they are often ignored or forgotten; their achievements trivialised in favour of their male counterparts. Virginia Woolf said that 'Anon, who wrote so many poems without signing them, was often a woman', and these words were steeped in truth. Many women found that it was easier to publicise their work as no one, than as a woman. It was easier to be taken seriously as an artist if they were nobody at all, instead of a girl.

Of course it was easier to be a man than to be nobody at all. The Brontë sisters from Yorkshire are famous for making their mark on classical literature under male pen-names: Currer, Ellis, and Acton Bell; for Charlotte, Emily, and Anne Brontë respectively.

On the Isle of Wight, and more than thirty years after the Brontë sisters published their first anthology (as the Bell brothers), a woman in Newport made the same choice. There were things that it was acceptable to write about as a female writer – books about the home, or beautifying oneself, or being the greatest mother – and there were things that were absolutely not considered feminine subjects at all. And Mary Gleed Tuttiett wanted to write about those. Her most well-known novel, *The Silence of Dean Maitland*, is about a churchman who killed somebody and allowed his friend to be wrongly imprisoned for the crime. Published in 1886, it was made into a stage play that had a successful run, and a film on three separate occasions: in 1914, in 1915, and in 1934. Two of Mary's other books were also made into films: *The Reproach of Annesley* in 1915, and *The Last Sentence* in 1917.

Mary's books were often romantic, and often laced with murder. While the former might've been excused, for women were considered whimsical, romantic readers (if permitted to read at all), the latter was definitely considered far too indelicate for a lady to be writing about. In order to be taken seriously by a publisher, and by the industry as a whole, it would have been easier for Mary to sell her manuscript as a man. She wrote under the pen name Maxwell Gray, and to this day is more famous as him than she is as herself.

In order to be taken seriously as a female artist, one would have to be incredibly robust, and determined, and self-confident. It's a competitive enough industry at the best of times, but their male counterparts would have had an advantage over them purely by being men. Even so, some women did pursue their career without adopting a pseudonym.

Enter Ellen Cantelo. Ellen was born in Carisbrooke on 13 April 1825, one of four siblings – two brothers (John and William), and a sister (Elizabeth). Elizabeth married a man called George Thompson and will be popping up again later on.

Ellen's father was a publican, running first The Castle and then The Eight Bells inns. He also made brushes. Ellen's brother John Cantelo is marked down on the 1851 census as a portrait painter. Ellen was a landscape and portrait painter on the same census, and living alone – although not too far away from the rest of the Cantelo family – on Carisbrooke Street.

By 1861, Ellen had moved to Millbrook Street – still in Carisbrooke. Her occupation was an 'artist in oil paintings', and she had taken on Elizabeth Froggatt, a 31-year-old schoolmistress, as a boarder. There were a number of schools in the area, including several that have since closed. It's likely that Elizabeth worked at one of these.

In the early 1870s, Ellen travelled up to London where she became a member of the Royal Society of Water Colourists. As a woman, this was the very best she could hope to do, as there were rules in place that prevented her from being accepted into the Royal Academy. This is a fine example of historical sexism at work; it was simply not acceptable for a woman to become a well-known artist and, as far as possible, there were measures in place to prevent it from happening.

Ellen eventually returned to the Isle of Wight, and to a house on Hope Street in Shanklin. When Elizabeth's husband passed away, she came to live with Ellen here.

Ellen dabbled in photography for a while, helping to establish the business of *Brading and Cantelo*. This duo took photographs all over the Island, some of which would go on to become postcards. By the time she died in 1898, Ellen had made quite the name for herself. She won awards and had made a living from her art. In her will, she left £253 to her sister Elizabeth (£19,778 today approx.).

Ellen Cantelo's work is going through something of a renaissance at the moment, and at the time of writing her name appears in several places celebrating Island celebrities. There is even a room named after her at the Isle of Wight Women's Centre in Newport.

It's probable that Ellen taught other Newport-born artist, Fanny Mary Minns. Fanny was approximately twenty years Ellen's junior, born in 1847, and incredibly fortunate in that her parents were the owners of a very lucrative company: *Bright and Minns* dry-cleaning and dyeing business. Bright was her mother's maiden name.

The Royal Academy opened its doors to women in 1862. Fanny elected to study her craft at Dresden Art Academy instead. She would return to Europe several times throughout her life, although continued to live with her mother on the Island once her education was complete. It's important to remember that as well as her natural talent, Fanny's financial situation made it possible for her to pursue a career as an artist. Ellen would never in her wildest dreams have been sent to study in Dresden as a young woman. The money simply wouldn't have been there for such an escapade.

As well as selling her paintings, Fanny worked as an art teacher to students on the Isle of Wight. She also took commissions; it was actually Fanny who did the artwork for Mary Gleed Tuttiett's *The Silence of Dean Maitland*. Her paintings won many awards and still fetch a decent price today. She passed away at the age of 82, and was buried alongside her mother in Mountjoy Cemetery in Carisbrooke.

As well as painting, another form of art aiming to capture the world around us was developed during this time period: photography.

Julia Margaret Cameron took up photography as a hobby when her daughter gave her a camera for her forty-eighth birthday in 1863. Her pictures are famous now for their unique style, the soft edges somehow helping to make the subject of the photo come to life before your eyes. Her models varied from her servants, to the people she spotted around her home in Freshwater, to family members and her elite circle of friends. Victorian celebrities often knew each other, whether because they were born into the nobility or because they were introduced by a shared acquaintance. Among Julia Cameron's photographs you'll find many familiar faces: Alfred Lord Tennyson (who was, after all, her neighbour), Charles Darwin, Sir John Herschel, Dame Ellen Terry. She also enjoyed recreating scenes from well-loved myths and historical stories.

Despite her illustrious clientele, Julia's work was not widely known until about 1948, when Helmut Gernsheim wrote a book about her career. He also noted, however, that she had left 'no mark' upon photography as a whole as her work had not been appreciated by her fellows, and thus not imitated.

One does have to wonder if perhaps she might've been taken more seriously were she a man, but I digress.

There have since been several exhibitions of Julia's work throughout various museums around the world, and her home in Freshwater has been transformed into a celebration of her life and work.

Elizabeth Sewell, already talked about in detail under *Education*, made her living as a writer. Her trademark stories for girls had a strong religious, moral core to them, although she also wrote nonfiction and historical works. When her father died in 1842, his children agreed to pay off his enormous debts. Much of this burden fell to Elizabeth, and she donated most of her earnings from her sales towards this endeavour over the course of the next thirty or so years, until the debts were vanquished completely. Her sister, Ellen Sewell, was an artist, known to enjoy sketching.

It's important to note that just because a woman did not make a career out of her art, that did not mean she wasn't very good at it. Many women throughout the Island's history, and especially at the height of its romanticism when the Victorians were flocking to its beaches in imitation of their queen, would have sought to capture its beauty. But most women would have painted, or played musical instruments, or sang, or danced, or written poetry, as a hobby. They would have been mother and wife foremost, and likely used their medium as a way to unwind at the end of a long, stressful day. But a person does not need to make a career out of their art, to be an artist. They just need to make the art in the first place.

# CHAPTER NINE

# Women and Crime

Some would have you believe that, once upon a time, it was inconceivable that a woman could possibly do something illegal; women were angelic human beings who stayed at home and kept house, and life would be much better if we could only go back to that. But don't be fooled. As long as there's been a law to break, you can bet that some woman, somewhere, was doing just that. That said, my adventures into the records detailing the arrests of citizens of the Isle of Wight from 1850 to 1950 have turned up a disproportionately large amount of men arrested compared to the number of women. Whether this means Island men were more badly behaved or just not as good in general at getting away with their crimes, we will never know.

Parkhurst Prison was very briefly an all-female prison in the 1860s. It was changed to house men in 1869, and everybody – inmates and staff – was moved up to the newly built Knaphill Prison in Woking, Surrey. Both before and after this decade, Island women who committed a crime deemed heinous enough to merit imprisonment would have to be shipped over to the mainland, if only because there was nowhere else to put them.

## Prisoners and Criminals

Scouring the prison records for our time period, we're faced with the sad fact that many of these women were arrested – and in many cases imprisoned – due to lack of access to legal, safe abortion methods. Women like Margaret Bay, who was acquitted of wilfully murdering her son Frederick, and then went on to marry less than three months later. It seems possible that Frederick was stillborn and her future husband was concerned, or perhaps that Margaret did try to kill him and was spared a sentence for lack of proof.

There are many women like Margaret. Indeed, one of the most common crimes women were tried for in this time period seems to be either 'wilfully killing her new-born child' or 'concealment of a pregnancy'. This meant not telling anybody that they were expecting a child, not reporting the birth, and not seeing the appropriate healthcare professionals to ensure that the pregnancy was going smoothly. It still happens today, particularly with teenage girls who fall pregnant by accident. This term also applied when a woman did not report a pregnancy because she didn't even realise that she was pregnant; while rare, this did happen.

Concealment of a pregnancy has been illegal in the UK since the 1861 Offences Against the Person Act, which stated: 'If any woman shall be delivered of a child, every person who shall, by any secret disposition of the dead body of the said child, whether such child died before, at, or after its birth, endeavour to conceal the birth thereof, shall be guilty of a misdemeanour,'. The wording here tells us that the crimes above were linked; that is, concealment of pregnancy often led to wilful murder of a new-born child. A person could be imprisoned for up to two years under this law.

The women being convicted of the above crimes were almost always unmarried, quite young and sometimes servants who would have been afraid to lose their job.

How scared must they have been?

The other crime that pops up time and time again is larceny, the penalty for which could be anything from six weeks' to eighteen months' imprisonment. Again, these were often young, working-class girls, quite possibly desperate for a bit of extra cash. The women accused of this often seem to be teenage girls; not really women at all, but children. Martha Harding was sentenced to fourteen days' imprisonment with hard labour followed by five years in a reformatory school for stealing money from one Ann Dashwood several times throughout the last four months of 1866 and passing it along to her mother. She was 14.

Alarmingly, women seem to pop up as victims of rape and assault with enormous frequency. Ann Kelleway, who was a 64-year-old mother of three boys and wife to a publican, was raped in Freshwater by a soldier in 1864. Her attacker was sentenced to seven years of penal servitude; he would have been shipped to Australia. It's heart-breaking to think that stories like Ann's were not uncommon, although at least she had the courage to come forward in pursuit of a prosecution, and at least her rapist was punished. Many more women would have slipped under the radar. It's likely that some of the girls prosecuted for killing their babies or concealing their pregnancies had been raped too, and then punished for it.

If you were hoping to read this chapter and learn of a hardened lady criminal from the Isle of Wight, though, then look no further than here. Allow me to introduce Mary Burt. Mary was born in Newport around 1848. In early 1869, Mary appears to have had her first run-in with the law. She was tried for stealing under the false name of Mary Thorn, and sentenced to four months' imprisonment.

Mary was in and out of various different prisons over the course of the next twelve years. The charges varied from being drunk, to being disorderly, to assault. In the May of 1872, she was sentenced to twelve months' imprisonment for being 'an incorrigible rogue and vagabond'. While in prison, Mary got into further trouble at least twice for arson; setting fire to her bedding, or to petticoats and clothing belonging to the prison.

All in all, it looks like Mary was arrested and tried a grand total of twenty-three times before 1882, when she was found guilty of 'maliciously wounding' a man. The list of her previous crimes at this hearing took up an entire page in the logbook! She was sentenced to five years' penal servitude. She was 34 at that time, at varying times marked down as a servant and a laundress, unmarried and presumably without children. And she'd been in and out of prison regularly since she was 21.

Penal servitude brings to mind ships full of convicts being sent to Australia, however this practice ended within the British Empire in 1868. Therefore, she would have been sent to a prison within UK borders. While there, she would be expected to work, often fulfilling hours of difficult labour every day without the promise of payment. Although originally intended to be useful to society as well as serve as a punishment for the convicted, by the time Mary was subject to penal servitude it had migrated to mostly being a method of breaking down a person's will. A common task given to female inmates, to give you a rough idea of the sort of things women like Mary would be expected to do, was 'oakum picking'. Oakum is a loose, fibrous material used to caulk boats; that is, plug holes and make the body watertight. It was deemed economical at this time to create oakum from recycled rope, which would need to be twisted loose by hand. The strands of the rope would then be unravelled into their separate fibres. This was arduous work, and often left hands ripped raw and bleeding.

Looking at cases of women like Mary, one would like to hope that, had she been born in the twenty-first century, we would give her the support she so clearly needed. Brutal, tedious tasks combined with forced solitary confinement can't have done her mental health any good. The last record I can find that seems to refer to our Mary has her marked down as 'M. B.' It's the 1891 census, and records the list of patients in the Hampshire County Lunatic Asylum, later known as Knowle Mental Hospital. It seems that the justice system finally gave up on Mary Burt, attributing her repeat offences to 'lunacy' and locking her away in another form of institution. The forced silence and solitary treatment of prisoners within the legal system causing mental health issues was not properly acknowledged until 1922.

## Careers Within the System

When creating a system that separates men from women, as the prison system in the UK has for over a century now, it makes sense to keep this in mind when hiring staff, too. Even in mixed gender prisons, the prisoners would be housed well away from each other, often in separate buildings, and would never interact.

Prior to this change in trend, jailers were often found charging prisoners for certain benefits: food, blankets, etc. Though this was made illegal in 1815, it does give you an idea of the power discrepancy between a prisoner and her jailer. It's not difficult to imagine situations where certain favours were asked for in exchange for the aforementioned benefits, in lieu of financial payment.

There were also firm gender roles in place throughout much of our time period; women would often be found in roles such as nursing or the prison kitchens, while men tended to be hired for the more managerial positions. Even so, for the most part, female officers were hired to work within female prisons, and men for male ones. Like many other traditionally male-dominated career paths, the prison system saw a sharp increase in female workers during and in the aftermath of the Second World War.

As mentioned above, Parkhurst was very briefly a female prison in the 1860s. Emily Jane Russell, one of five siblings born into a working-class background in Newport, probably began working there as an officer when she was in her teens. In 1869, Parkhurst was converted into an all-male facility, and the staff were transferred with the prisoners to the newly built all-female prison in Woking, Surrey. Emily must have been among them as on the 1871 census she is marked as living in Knaphill, Woking. She was working as a matron at this time.

Today, when we think of a matron, most of us will conjure up the image of a motherly woman in the medical profession; a nurse, old enough to have worked her way through the ranks and into a leadership role. However, in Emily's time the term was also used to describe a female prison warden, which has different connotations entirely. While she probably still retained the no-nonsense attitude of a senior nurse, Emily would have needed to be extremely strong, and firm, and possibly even a little bit scary.

Emily stayed at Knaphill Prison until 1896, when a number of female prisoners and staff were transferred to Aylesbury Gaol in Buckinghamshire. Among the prisoners was Florence Maybrick, who is famous to this day for being accused of poisoning her husband – himself a possible candidate for the notorious Jack the Ripper. Florence mentions in her memoirs that when she left Aylesbury Gaol in 1904, she was sad to say goodbye to some of the staff as well as her fellow prisoners; some of them had come up with her from Knaphill Prison, and thus she had spent the last fourteen or so years in their company. Emily would have been with Florence for most of this time, and was likely one of the matrons involved in this emotional farewell.

Emily worked as 'principal matron' at Aylesbury Gaol for some years, retiring in the early twentieth century. She had worked in the prison system for the entirety of her adult life, and was dedicated enough to rise up as far as it was possible for a woman to do. As principal matron, she would have been one of the most senior members of staff, supervising the lower-ranking matrons and overseeing the general running of the prison.

With a lack of female prisons on the Island, we also run into a lack of female staff within them. Emily Russell is a lovely, and rare, example of someone who started out at an early age not far from home, and then travelled across the Solent in pursuit of her career.

She never married, but she was living on a pension back in Newport when the 1911 census was taken.

# CHAPTER TEN

# Mental Health

While we have already touched on physical health issues a few chapters ago, this one shall focus on mental health. As I'm sure you've realised by now, understanding of mental health was not particularly at its best. A woman like Mary Burt mentioned in the last chapter would have been known as a rogue – a villainous pest who would likely learn the error of her ways if she received harsh enough punishment. And with mostly male doctors championing the medical profession, many issues women faced were simply brushed aside as her being silly and overly emotional. Now we're beginning to understand otherwise.

## Hysteria

This was a term used more in the first half of our time period to essentially dismiss a woman's fears or feelings, although it was still in use well into the 1900s in places. The dictionary definition of 'hysteria' today is an extreme or uncontrollable emotion: often excitement, but it can also mean anger, fear, anxiety – any emotion that can be heightened. The word actually stems from the Greek 'hystera', meaning 'uterus'. Which tells us all we need to know about who was typically being diagnosed with such a label.

Hysteria was a good way to invalidate anything a woman might say, as it would render her 'insane' and make it easy for one to claim that anything she said was the ramblings of a madwoman. If a husband, for example, wanted to do something his wife disagreed with, and had the necessary funds available, he could hire a doctor to come along and diagnose her with hysteria. Suddenly anything she had to say against his idea became irrelevant. She was insane. Hysterical.

Of course, some women diagnosed with hysteria genuinely did have a condition we would be able to recognise today. Many anxiety disorders, for example, might have been treated as hysteria 150 years ago. The overabundance of pure fear that comes with a panic attack might have been seen as hysteria. But at its very core, this diagnosis was a sexist one. It was viewed as a 'woman's disease'.

Unfortunately, hysteria is an argument we still see today when society seeks to invalidate a woman's position. We still have people claiming that women are 'too emotional' to run a business or a country. It's still easy to tell a woman who expresses any emotion at all that she's overreacting, which causes particular danger when it's used to guilt someone into keeping quiet in, say, a domestic abuse situation. We are coming to listen to the opinions of women in general more often, and to validate the emotions they might be feeling, but the binds of hysteria are proving difficult to break entirely.

On the Isle of Wight, we have a few cases of hysteria that made it into the papers – perhaps most tragically a woman named Frances Hurlock.

In June 1897, Frances committed suicide by jumping out of her bedroom window – a 35ft drop. She had been seeing a doctor for hysteria for the last two months. At the inquest, he explained that 'her taking up the study of anatomy' was the cause of her illness, and that she was 'over taxing her brain to study at the Art School'. Frances reportedly suffered several delusions, including one about how a member of the yacht club across the road from her house wanted to kill her cousin in the army. It appears from her father's testimony that they suspected she might be suicidal, as they took pains to ensure she was always accompanied if she ventured outside. She slept in the room beside his, and the Hurlocks took great pains to ensure all of the windows and doors in the house were locked. Sadly, she seems to have outwitted them somehow.

All of this was brushed under the rug as 'hysteria', when today we might instead have diagnosed someone suffering from similar symptoms to Frances with severe anxiety or depression, or perhaps bipolar disorder.

The 'Home Hints' section of a 1912 edition of the *Isle of Wight Times* offers advice for 'when a young girl becomes hysterical'. They stress that 'no show of sympathy' can be given. You must 'speak sharply to her before going out of the room and slamming the door behind'. They go on to say that if this seems too harsh, then 'the next best plan is to dash cold water over her and to hold very strong-smelling salts to her nostrils'. They then finish with a reminder that 'hysteria requires medical treatment'.

## Lunatics, Idiots, and Imbeciles

While these are all used as derogatory terms today, they were once used by the medical community to describe mental health conditions. In fact, there was a designated column on the census for recording whether or not a person was one of these things (as well as 'blind' or 'deaf and dumb', which are physical ailments and won't be covered here).

There was no fixed definition for any of these words until 1886, when the government passed the Idiots' Act. 'Lunacy' meant somebody who was mentally ill, unpredictable, and possibly dangerous. Anything from schizophrenia to bipolar disorder to generalised anxiety could be classified as such. 'Idiocy' was used to describe a person who had a mental age much younger than their physical one, and who was unable to protect themselves from certain everyday dangers. An 'imbecile' was incredibly similar, although a more extreme version. It's likely someone classified as this term would have had difficulty communicating verbally with others, for example.

On the 1901 census, all bar two of the female patients at Whitecroft Asylum in Newport were labelled as a 'lunatic'; 25-year-old E.G. was marked down as an 'imbecile', as well as 41-year-old L.H. from London. Mental institutions recorded patients on the census by their initials, as mental illnesses were still seen as something taboo, something embarrassing. This way their anonymity was preserved in some sense. It also made it harder to trace a patient back to their family, thus eliminating the risk of their name being tarnished.

The 1911 census provides a tiny bit more detail; the enumerator recorded the age at which each patient first began to show signs of their condition. A.W., for example, a 45-year-old milliner from Newport, first started showing signs of lunacy when she was 39. M.M. had been an imbecile since birth.

This makes it easier in some cases to make assumptions as to what a patient might actually be diagnosed with today. W.S. first started showing signs of 'lunacy' when she was 60. This means she was probably dealing with something that tends to affect the elderly – dementia, perhaps.

People could also find themselves in asylums for reasons we would now consider obscure. Lesbians and bisexual women would often find themselves being sent away to be 'cured' by their loved ones, who believed that their sexuality was a form of mental illness. Mental hospitals were also a wonderful place to send 'problem' women – girls who overheard something they shouldn't, perhaps.

## Post-natal Depression

Like many other 'women's problems', it's only recently that we have begun to talk about the effects this particular condition can have on a woman's life. This was a little understood malady, and while women today are lucky enough to have help available, the families of women during our time period who developed what we would now call post-natal or post-partum depression were often confused by their symptoms. Many found themselves placed in an asylum until they were deemed sane enough to go back home.

For example, Frances Mary Brown was admitted to the infamous Bethlem Royal Hospital in London (more commonly known as 'Bedlam') when she was 35. She had six children, the youngest being only 3 months old, and had suffered a prior attack of the same condition when she was 32. Her 'supposed cause of insanity' is marked down as 'suckling child'.

## Care

The Lunacy Act of 1845 stated that every county must have an asylum, whether of its own or shared with a neighbour. The Isle of Wight was still part of Hampshire at this time, and when building was completed on the Hampshire

County Lunatic Asylum in Knowle in the winter of 1852, this became the place for Islanders to send their mentally ill family members.

The site of this asylum was originally a farm, and part of the rehabilitation expected of patients was that they help keep it running. This is actually a surprisingly modern idea, with medical professionals today just beginning to realise the importance of giving people with certain disabilities something to focus on, or create, or do. They would still likely have been subject to the same treatments we view as utterly horrendous today, but they also had this small duty. And that was at least some sort of a step in the right direction.

There were over 400 patients at the asylum in 1856, and over 1,000 by 1900. By the end of 1950, there would have been almost 2,000 patients. However, since Whitecroft Asylum opened on the Isle of Wight in 1896, most Island women would have likely been sent there instead.

Plans for Whitecroft began in 1890, when the Isle of Wight became a county in its own right. Building began in 1894. There were to be four proposed blocks for the housing of patients, each two storeys high: one for recent cases; one for people with epilepsy; and one for chronic, but quiet and hard-working patients. There was also a designated block for the sick and bedridden, which would have housed patients such as those diagnosed with Generalised Paralysis of the Insane. This disease was a mystery at the time, and seemed to affect men more than it did women – although there were female sufferers, and several did end up in Whitecroft's wards. We now understand GPI to be the late stages of syphilis.

The very first patients to inhabit these wards were Islanders sent over from Knowle in 1896.

Male patients, as in Knowle, were given work to do around the farm. Women were taught skills such as knitting and basket-weaving. Weather permitting, some patients were allowed to venture outside of the grounds (under supervision) twice a week for 'exercise'.

As well as epilepsy and GPI, patients passed through Whitecroft with diagnoses of 'melancholia' – defined as an extended period of dejectedness, and very much a forerunner for modern day diagnoses of depression; and 'mania' – which is today associated with the higher feelings in a bipolar disorder, but back then could be used to refer to someone who was very happy, or very focused, or very distracted, or an insomniac. Mania seems to have been a great term for when you weren't actually entirely sure what was causing your patient's symptoms, but didn't want to admit that officially.

Cures throughout our time period were degrading for the patient to endure. Restraint was deemed completely okay, which might be understandable if somebody is posing a threat to themselves or others but would make a panic attack situation far worse. Controversial 'treatments' such as lobotomies and electroconvulsive therapy (ECT) were also introduced during our time period.

ECT became widespread in the 1930s, and initially began as a way to trigger convulsions in people with schizophrenia. It went on to be used for those diagnosed with depression too. Prior to this, medicine was ingested to trigger these convulsions instead.

The force of these convulsions was so severe that there were cases of patients breaking bones. As time progressed, mouth guards and body restraints were implemented in an attempt to combat this issue, as well as anaesthesia. ECT also had the unanticipated consequence of affecting the memories of some patients who endured it, making it difficult to judge whether or not they had actually ever consented to the treatment. ECT continued to be used throughout our time period, only being phased out in the 1960s.

A lobotomy is the practice of cutting into a person's skull and severing certain nerves. This was incredibly dangerous, and many people died as a result of it. Others survived but went on to commit suicide. As I'm sure you can imagine, snipping nerves within a system as complex as the human brain can be devastating. The idea behind the process was to make the patient less emotional, more docile and compliant. The emotions that tormented them would be erased completely, which is a wonderful thought when in the deepest depths of depression. But it would take away more than just the sadness; there were people who compared their loved ones to zombies when they returned. Some of them were unable to speak.

Prior to Whitecroft, and always an option for families who could not afford the fees it incurred, was the workhouse. The Isle of Wight House of Industry had a designated ward for the mentally ill, although it was far from a comfortable environment for them. Unsure how to handle people with often complex needs, staff were known to beat and abuse the people in their care. Nobody went to the workhouse to recover from their mental illness; they were put there because their loved ones could not cope any longer, and because they would die if they were left without any form of support.

# CHAPTER ELEVEN

# Women in Wartime

The First and Second World Wars would have affected everybody on the Island. It's difficult to picture the scale of it now, especially if you were born after 1945, but most of the men would not be there. Every woman would have had somebody she was praying for in the hope that it might help them return home to her safely, be that a husband, a son, a brother, or even just a friend. Even just the nice neighbour down the road whose cat liked to sleep in her garden; he'd be gone, too.

Conscription came into effect in March 1916 for the First World War, and October 1939 for the Second. By the end of 1939, over 1.5 million young men had been conscripted into the British armed forces; 1.1 million of them went on to join the British Army, and the remainder were split between the Royal Navy and the Royal Air Force.

Every single one of those 1.5 million men had left a home, family and friends. Every single one. It's estimated that the total number of widows made throughout the conflict in all participating countries was 3–4 million.

It's no surprise that many women wanted to assist with the war effort in any way they could. As mentioned in the *Leisure* chapter, there were groups of friends organising knitting parties so that they could send warm clothing to troops overseas. Many men in the trenches were especially grateful to receive food parcels from home, too, as their diet was famously atrocious and difficult to stomach. A tin of something sent over with love would have felt like a luxury.

With the Isle of Wight being so close to the continent (when compared to the rest of the UK), it was considered a potential target for enemy forces in both world wars. Being a tiny little island surrounded by ocean did rather put it at a disadvantage in that regard.

Blackout regulations came into force. Church bells were silenced and lights had to be switched off by a certain time, with penalties in place for those who refused to comply. There were also several people who apparently forgot about these new regulations, although whether or not this was actually true probably differed from case to case. Some children genuinely do forget to do their homework, some adults genuinely forget to send out birthday cards. Some of the more scatter-brained inhabitants of the Island were probably genuine in their mistake. Others probably latched onto the excuse in hope of a lighter sentence. It would have been incredibly easy to miss out a room when closing the blackout blinds at night, and the miniscule amount of light peeping through that one window would have been obvious to anybody walking past.

The Island was officially dubbed a prohibited area by the end of the First World War, and tourism wound down to a standstill. With so much of the Isle of Wight's income based around the tourism industry, this must've been a hard blow.

Many women struggled with raising the children alone while their husband was away fighting. There was a very real threat of being prosecuted for child neglect if they failed to make ends meet. One must remember that big families were still the norm when the First World War broke out, and it wasn't unusual to find one woman trying to care for, say, nine children on a soldier's wages. It isn't all that surprising that sometimes there wasn't enough food to go around, or enough money to spare for shoes that fit.

## Wives and Widows

We like to focus on the soldiers, particularly when talking about the First World War – and we certainly should remember their sacrifice – but war doesn't just affect the people who are fighting. It also affects the people they leave behind.

Most soldiers had a small percentage of their pay-cheque sent home to their wives if they were married. A little extra was sent if they had children together, although exact figures varied based on when in the war we're looking at and the position of the soldier in question.

The world didn't stop moving just because a war was going on. There were still children to care for, houses to keep, friends to meet, groceries to buy, and lives to live. As well as the usual demands of everyday life, women were met with new job opportunities, as already covered in the *Occupations* chapter.

While soldiers were granted leave, or could sneak home to see their families if they were stationed nearby (there were several military bases on the Island during the Second World War especially, and Portsmouth was always a busy naval hub), it was also entirely possible that a woman might only see her husband once or twice a year – and that was if she was lucky! Many soldiers were stationed further afield, and travelling home from overseas on a whim would have been much more difficult.

Of course, the warfront is a dangerous place to be, and many women received a telegram from the war office confirming the worst-case scenario; that their husband had died (or was missing in action, or a prisoner of war, and was presumed to be deceased – these were also sent out to families). What could a widow expect to happen to her at this time?

Firstly, she would be expected to go into mourning. It was considered highly inappropriate for her to jump into another relationship soon after receiving the news of her husband's misfortune. This period was expected of any widow, but it became especially important for war widows as their husband had died in service to the country. It would be disrespectful to his sacrifice if she moved on too quickly afterwards.

With the main breadwinner in the family gone, women were forced to find new ways to make ends meet. The government brought in the first non-contributory state pensions, meaning that widows of soldiers could receive a small amount of money without paying anything into it themselves; well, anything other than her husband's life, that is, which I'm sure many of them would have preferred to keep. Additional money was added to the pension amount for any children under the age of 16 dependent on the woman, or if she was suffering from a prolonged sickness that made it impossible for her to earn an additional income for herself.

The war widow's pension was notoriously small, and typically it wouldn't have been enough to live on. This, too, contributed to the influx of women taking up work in addition to raising their families. An advert in a 1919 edition of the *Isle of Wight Observer* reads: 'HOUSEKEEPER, war widow seeks situation as to working man: good references'.

That said, help was available on the Isle of Wight, with a regular New Year's party held at the large town hall in Ryde that was exclusive to war widows, their children, and the orphans living at Thornbury, a nearby church army home. The Ryde Relief Society also ran a soup kitchen, which many war widows no doubt relied on.

If a woman remarried, her pension was terminated. The expectation was probably that her new husband would be able to keep her fed, sheltered and clothed without need of it. That, and many men did not like the thought of their wives being married previously. A regular pension would have been a constant reminder that she'd had a lover who had fought and died and probably broken her heart, before she'd ever made any vows to be faithful to her new husband.

## Rationing

Compulsory rationing was only introduced for the First World War in 1918; the war ended in 1919. Prior to this, it was a highly encouraged but optional undertaking that a lot of people chose to ignore.

Perhaps this late introduction is why we tend to associate the practice more with the Second World War. In both cases, however, a range of variables – from the majority of the farmers and labourers signing up to fight, to the threat of enemy submarines and mines in the English Channel – led to a need to conserve the food we had, and to become less reliant on imported goods.

Women across the country adapted everyday recipes to fit in with the new rationing scheme while still managing to keep their families healthy and well fed. Indeed, it's generally believed that people were much healthier during wartime because they ate fewer unhealthy foods than we do today and instead consumed a lot more vegetables, which could be easily grown at home.

It also meant that most households threw out a lot less waste than we do today. Anything that could be recycled, would be. Vegetable off-cuts and peelings would be boiled together at the end of the week to make a stew. The leftover pieces from a hunk of meat (the bones, tissues, sinewy parts etc.) would be stripped bare and turned into soup. Stale bread became bread-and-butter pudding. Potatoes, which could be grown more-or-less anywhere and were thus one of the nation's more abundant resources, were used for cakes and scones as well as for dinner. Carrot cakes were a historical dessert that was revived again during the war, as the carrot's natural sweetness meant less sugar was needed to make something that tasted indulgent to eat.

Mothers worked out how to fake things; how to make cakes without eggs, how to make 'cream' with butter and sugar, how to fake the taste of bananas using parsnips. Fruits such as bananas were impossible to get hold of during the war, as they can only be grown overseas where the climate is warmer. Prior to the war, though, these fruits became beloved of the British public, and so were sorely missed. It's only natural that people would seek out alternatives.

On the next page is a recipe for toffee. My great-grandmother, Fif Toogood, used to make sweets for her children during the war, as these were rationed along with everything else. Although her original recipe has been lost to time, I've tried my best to recreate it. The recipe is based around one first published after the Second World War, but I've played around with the ingredients and measurements so that they are compatible with rationing. It would have been possible to make this toffee, and still have some of your butter/margarine and sugar rations left over to see you through the rest of the week.

## TOOGOOD TOFFEE

60g margarine (butter is ideal, but the ration for this was only 50g per week for an adult! Margarine, however, was set at 100g)

50g sugar (was rationed at roughly 225g per week)

2 tbsp golden syrup

1 tin of condensed milk (375g)

1. Line or grease a tin. I prefer to use a smaller tin, although if you like your toffee thin use a larger one.
2. Put everything except the condensed milk in a large, heavy-bottomed pan. Heat, stirring continuously, until all the sugar has dissolved.
3. Add the condensed milk.
4. Bring to the boil. Keep stirring. If left, it will burn; and even if only a tiny fraction of the mixture does burn, it will affect the taste of the whole batch.
5. When it reaches 'hard ball' stage, remove from the heat. If you're using a sugar thermometer, this should be around 121° Celsius. If you are not using a thermometer, this temperature is called the 'hard ball' stage because if you drop a small amount of the mixture into cold water, it should form a hard ball that holds its shape when you take it out – although still soft enough to squish and mould with your fingers. In your pan, it should drip from your spoon in thick, rope-like strands.
6. Pour into your prepared tin and leave to cool.
7. Once it has cooled slightly, mark into squares. You'll want to do this otherwise you'll end up with one huge lump of toffee!
8. Leave to cool completely – overnight is best. You can put it in the fridge if you'd like, although if we're being

entirely traditional, just pop it somewhere relatively cool. A pantry would be good if you have one.

9. Break up along the lines you marked earlier.
10. Enjoy!

Please note that confectionary can be difficult to master, so practise, practise, practise. I'm sure that my great-grandmother's first few batches came out rather interesting, too. Thankfully, even failed attempts at toffee still taste delicious; and if it's too soft to eat as a sweet on its own, it goes excellently with ice-cream!

Sometimes, through clumsiness or forgetfulness, or even just sheer bad luck, ration books were misplaced. This made it incredibly difficult to buy groceries until a replacement was sent out. In August 1918, during the First World War, the *Isle of Wight Observer* ran a rather amusing little story. Mrs L. Burden (possibly Emily Burden, who was married to a sailmaker named Lewis) sent one of her children out on 'a food errand', giving them their older sister's ration book (if this is indeed Emily Burden) and sending them off to buy groceries. This was not an uncommon occurrence, and mothers often sent children out to run errands such as this. While the little Burden was otherwise occupied (we don't know how old the child was), 'a wandering and presumably hungry donkey' put its head in their basket and stole Miss B. Burden's ration book (Emily's daughter Beatrice would have been in her twenties, hence why it seems unlikely she is the child the story is referring to. Her youngest sibling as of the 1911 census, however, would have only been six or seven), eating a whole quarter's worth of ration coupons before the child managed to get the book back. The *Observer* explained that Beatrice had, understandably, 'been put to some inconvenience' in her attempts to reclaim the lost coupons, and that in the mean-time the family 'have had to "go shares"'.

As well as foods, clothing was also rationed as the resources required to make the fabric (e.g. cotton, silk) were rarely grown and produced in the UK. This meant that people would have tried to make the clothes they did have last as long as possible. Holes were patched up, buttons were replaced – and not always with one that matched that which had been lost! It was either this, or wander around naked, which probably wasn't very appealing to most women in the 1940s. It's not especially appealing now, I would wager.

Of course, if you wanted more than your weekly ration, there were ways and means to achieve this. None of these were technically legal, but most mothers will go to great lengths to feed their children. That, or she might want a little more of a given food if she was expecting guests, or if it was a special occasion; perhaps her husband was expected home on leave soon, or it was somebody's birthday.

Whatever it was, some local shopkeepers were willing to part with any leftover stock they might've had. This service was incredibly expensive, however, and the penalty if caught would likely be an incredibly hefty fine. There were also cases of people using the tokens from more than one ration book. For example, when a relative died, rather than hand their used ration book over to the authorities, it was kept and used as a supplement to the ones already owned by the family.

Referring back once again to that idea of women looking out for their neighbours, it also wasn't uncommon to swap goods. Say, for example, you really wanted to bake a cake, but were an egg short. You might ask a friend to give you one of hers in exchange for, say, half your week's ration of milk. You might also have one friend who gets through a lot of cheese, but you and your family don't particularly care for it. In which case you might swap your weekly ration of cheese in exchange for something of hers she won't use. This kind of behaviour was also technically illegal, but it was difficult to trace as the women would still be using their own coupons, and the right amount at that. The cheese just ended up in someone else's kitchen.

Fish and game animals (rabbits, deer, etc.) were not rationed at all, which meant that if you could (legally) catch them, they were yours! I imagine a lot of children on the Island would have found themselves eating fish for dinner quite a bit during the war, since it's rather an abundant resource. There are up-sides to being on a tiny little island surrounded by soldiers in the middle of a very big war. That said, poaching seems to have been a regular issue in the early 1900s regardless of whether or not there was a war on, and many people – usually young men or teenage boys – were arrested for it.

## Threats from Overseas

Wartime Britain was a scary place to live – wailing air-raid sirens, bombs falling from the sky, the possibility you might never see your loved ones again each time you parted. The Isle of Wight was no exception.

There were army barracks dotted around the Island, and coastal defences were set up to make it more difficult for boats to land on the shore. Furthermore, there were mines buried on most beaches on the Island, and access to these for the public was heavily restricted. This would have been a bizarre turn of events for a community of people who had always had ready access to the ocean in years past. There was a small strip of beach that could be used by locals and military personnel, but that was all.

And of military personnel, there were plenty! As well as the men being housed in the barracks in case they were needed, there were soldiers using the Island as a training ground – particularly during the Second World War. Depending on whereabouts you lived, there would have been times when you could probably scarcely leave your house without bumping into somebody from the armed forces!

There were, of course, many stories of Island girls being swept off their feet by dashing soldiers stationed locally. Most of them had happy endings, with the two of them surviving the war and enjoying long, loving relationships lasting well into old age. Yes, there would have been all kinds of health issues due to the war – both mental and physical – but they endured. Because they were in love, and that's what you do when you love somebody; you help each other through the rough patches so that you can enjoy the niceties together.

Some stories, however, were tragedies. Edith May Toogood (at that time in her life, she liked to be called 'May'. Later she became known as 'Fif' – it's her toffee recipe I tried to recreate earlier in this chapter) fell in love with a navy seaman called Charles Samuel Bennett. They married in 1916, when she was only 19, and he continued to work with the Royal Navy. By the summer of 1917, May was pregnant with Charlie (Charles Bennett jnr), although only a month or two. We don't know if she even knew she was with child when the news reached her that her husband had been killed. His ship, the HMS *Tartar*, struck a mine off the coast of Boulogne and had to be towed back to Portsmouth. Charles died of his injuries shortly after the explosion.

If May hadn't realised she was pregnant when Charles died, she would have discovered it within the next few weeks. This would have been a terrifying time for her, racked with grief having lost her first love and then suddenly discovering that she would have to raise a baby by herself. She might even have considered the extreme abortion methods mentioned in the *Health* chapter, although if so, she did not go through with any of them.

Charles was from Portsea, just across the Solent, and May was an Island girl through-and-through. Living in Newport, she would have been surrounded by family. Her older sister Florence had a husband fighting in Iraq around this time with the Mesopotamian Expeditionary Forces. Their mother, Alice Fuller, was known to act as a midwife should she be needed, although this was never an official job of hers. She may well have been the one to deliver Charlie Bennett in early 1918, although this would have been slightly illegal if so, as midwives were required to be trained and certified by this time.

Florence's husband, Walter Burrell, died the October of that year during the Battle of Sharqat. She remarried on Christmas Day 1919; another soldier, Percival Stay, survived the war, and the couple moved up to Surrey with May when she left in pursuit of a career as a nanny, possibly because the recent experiences she'd had on the Island had left her hurt and in need of a change. This would have been soon after the February of 1923, as this was when Charlie died of catarrhal jaundice. He was only 5 years old. His uncle, the husband of May's sister Elsie, was the informant; it seems likely that May, in her grief, had been unable to bring herself to do it. Perhaps Elsie elected to stay with her while her husband handled the paperwork.

May remarried in 1924; a carpenter named Thomas Hayton. They went on to have four children together: Pamela, Patricia, Reginald, and Roy. May moved back to the Island when the children were all grown. Thomas, although offered the chance to join her, declined and remained in Leatherhead. May lived in her family's home on Clarence Road in Newport until her death in 1976. Her two sons also moved down there post-retirement, with Roy living close to her old stomping ground at the time of writing, with his wife and youngest son.

# CHAPTER TWELVE

# Suffrage

The 'suffrage movement' as we know it was founded by Millicent Garrett. Its goal? Convincing the government that women deserved the right to vote. It can be hard to picture for some of us alive in the UK today, but it was only a century ago that women were even granted this right in our country. While we like to imagine that our own ancestors were at the forefront of political changes, the pinnacle of bravery, and among the most just and righteous people of their time, the sad truth is that most of us probably cannot rightfully claim such things.

To support women's suffrage was scandalous. And in a time when most women were expected to agree with their husband's every word, I'm sure you can imagine how the majority viewed such a scandal.

Views on the Isle of Wight seem to have been rather anti-suffrage throughout the time that the movement was rocking the mainland. The prevailing view was that supporters of the movement were unhappy, unmarried, ugly old ladies, and that the majority of women were satisfied with the way things were. While there were probably a few women who did support the suffrage movement on the Island, it's likely that they were afraid to be vocal. Mob mentality is a very real thing, and the fear of being ostracised, penalised, and hated by the people close to them was more than most women could bear. So while they might have agreed privately, their outward projection to the world would mirror the views of their husbands and fathers; they would condemn the suffrage movement aloud.

And then there were the women who would have disagreed with the movement both inside and out. They would have believed in the anti-suffrage propaganda, and found it difficult to understand why these other women seemed so upset. These were women who had found happiness as mothers and wives, or hoped to do so in the future; women who genuinely believed that all others of their gender must aspire towards the same ends. Suffragettes and suffragists must simply not know the joys of motherhood, of being a good wife. They were bitter and resentful, and wanted to go against the natural order of things by rising up to the same level as the men in their lives. And why should they want that?

A poll was conducted in 1911 of '611 lady municipal voters at Ryde on the desirability of votes for women'. Only 55 of these women voted 'for'; 191 voted 'against'; 365 voted 'undecided'. Colonel Hamilton, who conducted this poll, 'ask[ed] where the Suffragette assertion that wise women want to vote comes in'. This seems rather like a slight against the fifty-five ladies who voted 'for'.

All that said, the Isle of Wight can boast three born-and-bred suffragists, around when the campaign for women's votes first began. Suffragists were not militant, as the suffragettes were. Founded before their more aggressive sisters, the suffragists wanted to win the vote peacefully and legally, without hurting anybody, and without violence of any sort.

In 1886, John Stuart Mill MP agreed to present a petition pertaining to the matter of women's suffrage to Parliament if it managed to garner at least 100 signatures. The final number gained was 1,521.

Of those signatures, three came from the Isle of Wight; Ellen Cantelo's, Elizabeth Thompson's, and Sarah James's.

Ellen will already be a familiar figure if you've been paying attention thus far. She was the award-winning painter mentioned in the *Arts* chapter, and in 1866 she would have been 41.

Elizabeth Thompson was her little sister. Unlike the stereotype – as well as the other two Island suffragists recorded on the petition – she was married. George Thompson was a coachmaker, and on the 1871 census they were living on Union Street in Newport. After his death in 1888, she moved in with her sister in Shanklin and took up work as a stationer.

The third name, Sarah James, seems to have belonged to Ellen and Elizabeth's maternal aunt. Sarah, like Ellen, never married. She also doesn't seem to have had a fixed address, lodging with a different family in a new house with every census taken. She worked as a milliner for most of her adult life, switching to dressmaker with the 1871 census, and 'formerly dressmaker' with the 1881 one.

The names on the 1866 petition were mostly gathered by people spreading the word to their circle of friends and their families, who would then spread the word to their own, and so on and so on. It therefore makes sense that the three suffragists on the Island were related to each other. Probably one heard about the petition and informed the other two, and they agreed to send their signatures up to the mainland for it together. But which of them got the ball rolling?

My suspicion is that it was Ellen Cantelo. We know that she had friends in London, where the suffrage movement was much stronger than it ever was on the Island. Artists have always had a reputation for being among the frontrunners wherever change is involved; it's their job to document the world around them, the way it changes, the way it used to be before. I therefore think it most likely that Ellen learned of it from her artsy Londoner friends, told Elizabeth and Sarah, and it went from there.

The petition containing their names was taken to Parliament by Elizabeth Garrett and Emily Davies, where it was presented by John Stuart Mill as he had promised. He argued that the entire endeavour had been organised exclusively by women, which must surely go to show how much they wanted to be granted their right to vote. This was the first time the issue had been discussed in Parliament.

The first parliamentary debate regarding this matter occurred the following year, in 1867. John Stuart Mill worked with many other politicians who also felt women deserved the vote, including Henry Fawcett who would marry a young woman named Millicent Garrett that year. Millicent Garrett Fawcett was a frontrunner for the campaign of women's suffrage, and helped to found and to run the suffragist movement. She was involved heavily with Henry and John's work that year, along with her sister, Elizabeth (the same Elizabeth who presented the petition the year before).

In the end, the motion lost; 73 votes to 196. However, it remains a crucial moment as it was this petition, this debate, that got parliament talking about giving women the vote. It was this moment that women throughout the UK who had perhaps not seen the initial petition, or not believed it would be seriously considered, began to question why they weren't granted the same rights as their husbands, brothers, fathers.

The House of Commons and the House of Lords went on to receive over 16,000 petitions pertaining to the issue of women's suffrage between 1866 and 1918, and it's entirely possible that some Island women pop up on those. The very next one was presented shortly after that first failed debate, in 1868.

As well as these three women, over the course of the suffrage campaign others would come forward with their own ideas and their own ways of fighting. The majority of the violence, however, does not seem to have reached the Isle of Wight. Women's suffrage supporters remained in the minority even at the height of the movement, and they seem to have remained suffragists – never suffragettes.

Women were finally granted the vote in 1918, provided they were over 30 years old and owned at least a minimum quantity of property. They were not placed on equal footing with men until 1928.

# Acknowledgements

You never quite appreciate how many people it takes to get a book ready to go until you're creating one yourself. *A History of Women's Lives on the Isle of Wight* required a small army to come into existence, and I'd like to take a moment to thank a few of the people who were a part of it. To thank each and every one of you would take an entire book on its own and, though I would be more than happy to write such a book, I doubt it would make for a riveting read.

First things first, I'd like to thank the Pen & Sword team. In particular; thank you Roni for taking a chance with me; thank you Heather for helping with my earlier edits; and thank you Amy for being the most understanding editor a writer could hope for.

Thank you Karyn for making this book somewhat legible. Goodness knows, you've saved me from looking completely ridiculous in places.

Thank you to Auntie Pat (Pat Channon) for your lovely long letters and emails about my great-grandmother, and for the photographs, and the stories. Thank you Granddad (Roy Hayton) for all your wonderful anecdotes, and for letting me stay with you.

Thank you to Chloe Bryant for traipsing around the Island with me on a few particularly rainy days one May in search of photo opportunities and interesting facts to include.

Thank you Jack Howes for your absolutely beautiful picture of an old Isle of Wight cottage. I'm always left a little star-struck by your artwork, and this one was no exception.

Thank you to Anna and Cela from Portsmouth University, who provided me with a great deal of information about its life before it was granted university status.

Thank you to Kenneth Florey for his cooperation, and his vast collection of suffrage memorabilia. And thank you to Geoff Allan of the Isle of Wight Family History Society, for allowing me to use his photograph of the Sewell sisters' plaque in Bonchurch.

# Resources

www.the1940sexperiment.com

www.ancestry.co.uk

Ann Barrett (www.annbarrett.co.uk)

www.avjobs.com/history

www.awesomestories.com

www.bbc.co.uk

www.blackgangchine.com

www.bonchurchvillage.co.uk

British Newspaper Archive

Cambridge Family Law Practice (www.cflp.co.uk)

Culture24

Department of Education, National Statistics, Pupil Absence in Schools in England autumn 2016 – spring 2017

www.fashionhistory.fitnyc.edu

www.findmypast.co.uk

Early Office Museum (www.officemuseum.com)

https://encyclopedia.1914-1918-online.net/article/war_widows

English Heritage (www.english-heritage.org.uk)

FPA The Sexual Health Charity (www.fpa.org.uk)

*The Guardian*

*Huffington Post*

www.iowhospitals.org.uk

www.isle-of-wight-memorials.org.uk

www.jantoms-brief-biographies.com

Keith Harcourt and Roy Edwards, The Science Museum Group Journal, article citation: 10.15180; 1851009

Kirsty Stonell Walker (www.fannycornforth.blogspot.com)

www.legislation.gov.uk

Lucey, Donna M., *Sargent's Women: Four Lives Behind the Canvas.* (W.W. Norton & Company, 2017)

The Metropolitan Museum of Art

Money Week

The Old Thatch Teashop (www.oldthatchteashop.co.uk)

www.onaverage.co.uk

www.ourworldindata.org

Oxford Royale

www.parliament.uk

Portsmouth University

www.sciencebasedmedicine.org

The Science Museum

Sewell, Eleanor L. & Elizabeth Missing, *The Autobiography of Elizabeth M. Sewell* (Longmans, Green, 1907)

Sudni Heritage blog

www.suffolkartists.co.uk

Trow, M.J., *Foul Deeds and Suspicious Deaths on the Isle of Wight* (Pen & Sword, 2009)

Vacuum Cleaner History (www.vacuumcleanerhistory.com)

www.victorianweb.org

www.waywardwomen.wordpress.com

www.wightatwar.org.uk

www.wokingprison.blogspot.com

www.womensuffragememorabilia.com

# Index